CW01183134

DELIUS KLASING

AUDI TT

Written by
Jürgen Lewandowski   David Staretz   Herbert Völker

Photographed by
Peter Vann

DELIUS KLASING VERLAG

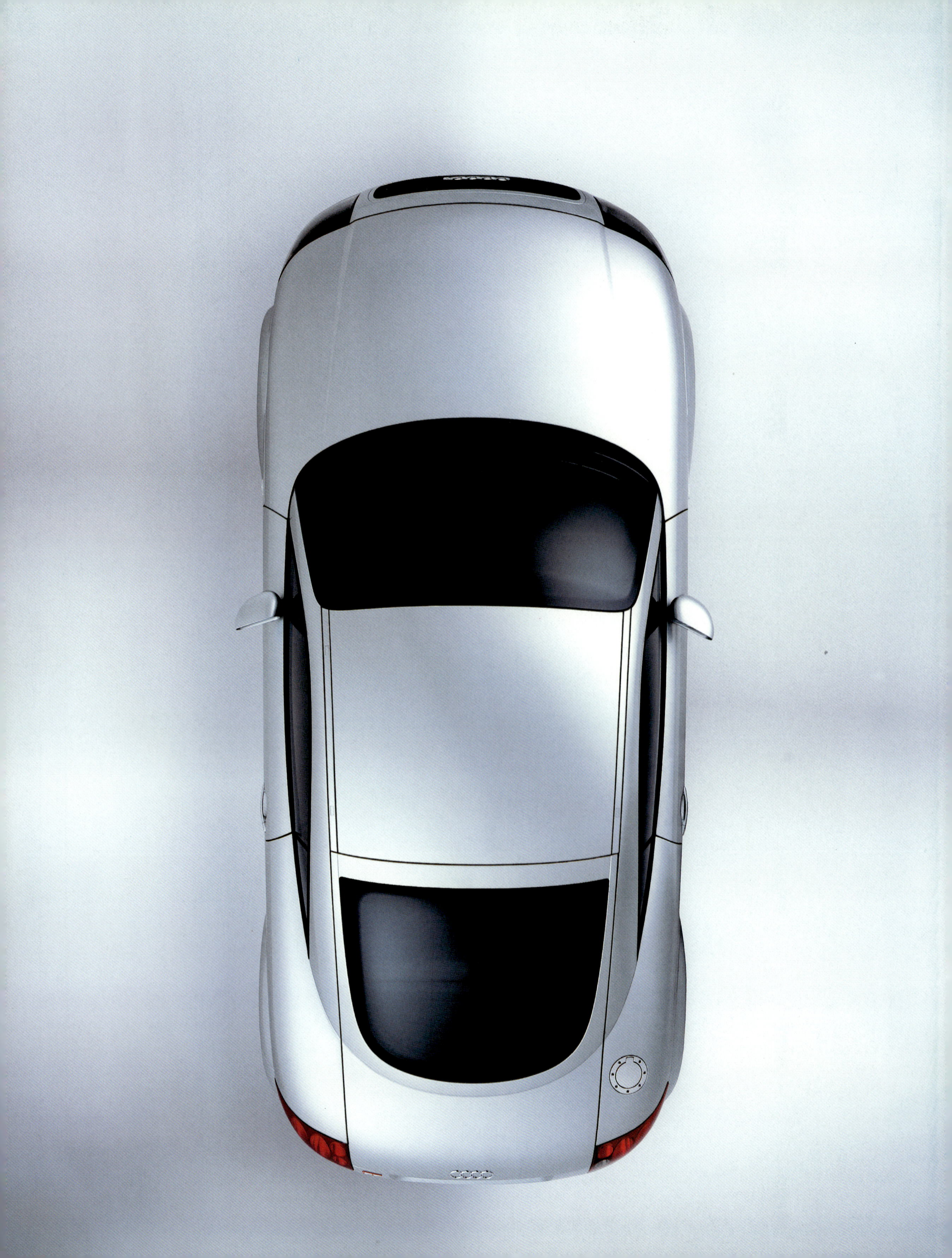

Contents

SIGNS 10 — An interview with Dr. Franz-Josef Paefgen

DESIGN 16 — In the Beginning was the Idea

TECHNICAL 42 — Making the car mobile

PRODUCTION 70 — The TT is always on the move

A TT is a TT **78**
APPEARANCE

The making-of-story of the introductory photos
ICELAND 90

112 The car that loves the city
PARIS

FACTS 126
Performance that can be Measured

What Takes Your Fancy?
LIFESTYLE 134

Interview

A Dramatic Statement

An interview with Dr. Franz-Josef Paefgen

Dr. Paefgen was interviewed by Jürgen Lewandowski

ONE DOESN'T OFTEN GET TO SPEAK for any length of time to the president of a large motor-vehicle manufacturer, one of the men who hold the destiny of a company in their hands. You have to wait endlessly for a blank space in their appointments calendar, which is booked up way ahead. And you have to make sure you raise some interesting subjects and questions. Otherwise, they may regret making time to speak to you.

Of course, often-asked questions do have their attraction: they are a good opportunity to add to a well-established foundation, like extending a house or adding a bay window to give it a new look.

What does the TT mean for Audi?
(For the President of Audi AG, Dr. Franz-Josef Paefgen, this first question offers a welcome opportunity to put the TT Coupé and the TT Roadster in a historical context right from the outset.)

If you consider Audi's past, you'll see that it undoubtedly divides into two main periods. First of all, there was the period initiated and shaped by Dr. Piëch, in which the marque redifined itself by introducing new technologies and rigorous quality standards. Innovations such as the quattro driveline, TDI engines and the use of aluminium ensured that, over the years, Audi's name became increasingly synonymous in the public mind with advanced engineering.

This was followed by a second phase, in which emotion was introduced into the equation, in parallel, naturally, with further developments on the engineering side. With powerful and distinctive advertising and a design standard that set Audi increasingly apart from the rest, it built up a fund of goodwill – a feel-good factor – around the engineering that clearly benefited the company.

The TT represents a powerful statement to round off this second phase. At the same time, we are entering new territory that will eventually form the basis for the third phase of Audi's development.

Given that you see the TT as a powerful statement and a step into new territory, how do you explain the willing acceptance of the company in this new role? You had the entire motoring world at your feet after the first two TT studies.

I think the secret is that for many years now Audi has been thinking in a long-term way. In Ingolstadt, we don't take decisions overnight. We don't change our strategy for the sake of short-term gain. The only successful strategy is a long-term one – and evidently the time was right for the TT. Or, to put it another way, nothing is more powerful than an idea when its time has come.

"The TT sums up everything our company is trying to achieve: high-technology and design, 'Vorsprung durch Technik' and a challenge to the conventional."

"The TT was developed at a time of extremely rapid change in the positioning of all roadsters then under development."

There was a time once before when this idea's time seemed to have come – did the quattro spyder of 1992 just arrive too early on the scene, when the field was unfamiliar and ill-defined?

This study, which was mourned for a long time, had one major defect.
Because all the components had been designed from scratch, Audi would have had to reach deep into its own pocket for every one it sold, even if the price (in terms of German marks) had been in six figures. To look at the situation more positively: the quattro spyder taught us that we would have to take a different approach to the roadster and coupé concept – namely on the basis of existing technology that would enable us to charge a reasonable price and, as a result, achieve the appropriate production volume.

New models are always associated with the company as a whole. Given the thousands of engineers and gigabytes of computer capacity involved, is it still possible to think of individuals defining, drafting out and implementing a car? Who were the "fathers" of the TT? In view of the teamwork involved, is it still possible to think in terms of individuals writing automotive history?

Large companies in particular rely on individuals to a far larger extent than the public would ever imagine. And the fact that the TT exists today comes down ultimately to just two people:

The first was Dr. Ulrich Hackenberg, who came into my office one day with a couple of drawings and some calculations for an A3 platform with a shortened wheelbase and said that the idea was perfectly feasible. And it was he who, as project co-ordinator, subsequently brought together the designers and engineers and reconciled their differing notions of what was imaginative, attractive and feasible.

The second person was the American designer, Freeman Thomas, who pulled off the remarkable feat of creating a truly unmistakable form on the basis of an existing technical platform. These two are the "fathers" of the TT – their colleagues were the "midwives", who also actively contributed to the success of the project.

When was the decision to build the TT taken?

As I have already said, we had learned from the unfortunate demise of the quattro spyder, so we already knew when the TT design study was first shown at the Frankfurt Motor Show that it made sense financially. The huge success of the TT's appearances in Frankfurt and Tokyo was in fact just final confirmation that the decision to put it into production was correct. Of course, we also commissioned a number of market research studies from independent organisations, and they gave us a clear message: build it!
Put simply, we had learnt our lesson. So ultimately the cancellation of the quattro spyder was a stroke of luck when it came to the TT.

Even so, it took longer than expected to get into production.

The TT was developed at a time of extremely rapid change in the positioning of all the roadsters then under development. It was also a time when rival manufacturers were trying to outdo each other's performance figures.

Just as BMW had to add a six-cylinder to the existing four-cylinder engines for its Z3 and Mercedes decided on a supercharger for its SLK, the TT went through a major transformation within an extremely short time. Originally, it was intended to have a power output of 150 bhp but it ended up with 180 and 225 bhp versions, in other words a 50% increase in the power output from the starting point to today's top model. As a result, almost all the components had to be modified, from the engine and running gear to the steering and brakes. Changes like that can't be designed, tested and set up for series production in just a few weeks. It takes time.

Why is the TT called the TT? Or was the name clear right from the outset?

Normally, naming a new model is well down the list of priorities. Up to that point, it's generally given a code name for internal use. This makes communication within the company easier and also helps to keep it a secret, at least for a limited time.

As with all new models, there were numerous suggestions for the TT. Some of them were meant to be serious, others less so. Freeman Thomas, for instance, who incidentally liked to turn up at the design studio during the period of work on the TT in leather shorts and a traditional hat, came up with two slightly eccentric suggestions: The Gaimersheim (a small suburb of Ingolstadt) and the Audi Edelweiss. Perhaps it was the edelweiss on his hat that gave him the idea – I don't know.

Freeman Thomas is also credited with the phrase "This car speaks German". Nevertheless, they didn't play German folk music while they worked. It was mostly Jimi Hendrix.

These very unusual names weren't taken seriously into consideration. Ultimately, a number of more prosaic ones were presented to the Board: C3 or A3 C, for example, standing for Audi A3 Coupé. The letters TT were also discussed but were initially dropped from the list of suggestions because to many they seemed too close to the old NSU tradition. And you don't really want to associate a completely new car with a bygone era.

In the end, we agreed on the name Audi A3 C – but just a week later the project team came to the next meeting of the Board and asked if it could be changed to TT after all. Although we were a little surprised, we finally agreed and it obviously wasn't a bad decision.

Interview

On show in Tokyo
"Once the Coupé and the Roadster had had their premiere in Frankfurt and Tokyo and the green light had been given for series production, we got the Coupé ready for the road, though not without some difficulty."

When was the first time you really felt sure about the car?

When we saw the first two quarter-scale models in the design studio, I felt convinced that it would be a hit. Once the Coupé and the Roadster had had their premiere in Frankfurt and Tokyo and the green light had been given for series production, we got the Coupé ready for the road, though not without some difficulty.

And when we drove the TT on our test track in Neustadt for the first time and saw it in the open air, next to other cars, when its unusual proportions and forms showed up to advantage in comparison with the competition, I was sure that we were on the right track with the TT. It embodied Audi's competence in design like no other model before it.

Of course, the TT's design led to a sharp polarisation of opinion and to arguments right from the start between people with opposing points of view, and the comments covered the whole gamut from "some kind of mad armoured reconnaissance vehicle" or "Alessi toaster on wheels" to "the most substantial Audi there's ever been". Mobile proof of a passion for motor cars

Interview

Nothing less than mobile proof of Audi's passion for the motor car.

On that day in Neustadt, these comments had not yet been made, but somehow they were very much in the air. This is perhaps because the TT sums up everything our company is trying to achieve: high technology and design, 'Vorsprung durch Technik' and a challenge to the conventional. At that moment on the approach lane, the car proved that we weren't just anybody – we were unmistakably Audi.

And with its sense of presence, it convinced everybody there, including me.

The term "sports car" naturally implies the concept of sport – as in motor sport. Will the TT be given an opportunity to show what it can do in that department?

A car's success in motor sport is closely tied up with its potential within the framework of the regulations, so first of all you have to take a close look at them. Unfortunately you will then find that the TT has no chance of entering any of the existing motor sport categories.

And since Audi would never invest either financial resources or personnel in a project if it has no realistic chance of winning, I don't see any prospect at present of the TT being entered for motor racing events. One alternative would be a one-make manufacturer's cup. But it's doubtful whether it would be all that attractive to have a lot of TT's competing against each other. The idea in motor sport is to win against the competition.

There's only one possible conclusion: of course, the TT is a classic GT and there would be opportunities for it to demonstrate its special qualities there, but unfortunately there is no category it could enter according to the regulations.

And what would be your final word on the TT?

Just under two decades after the original quattro, which made motor sport and engineering history with its four-wheel drive system, turbocharged engine and 200 bhp power output, the TT is continuing the Audi story in its own way. However, whereas in the past the desire to write engineering history was cloaked in a somewhat modest exterior, the passion for technology (that still exists) is now wrapped in a distinctive design that stirs the emotions.

In the final analysis, whether in open- or closed-top form, this car is nothing less than mobile proof of Audi's passion for the motor car.

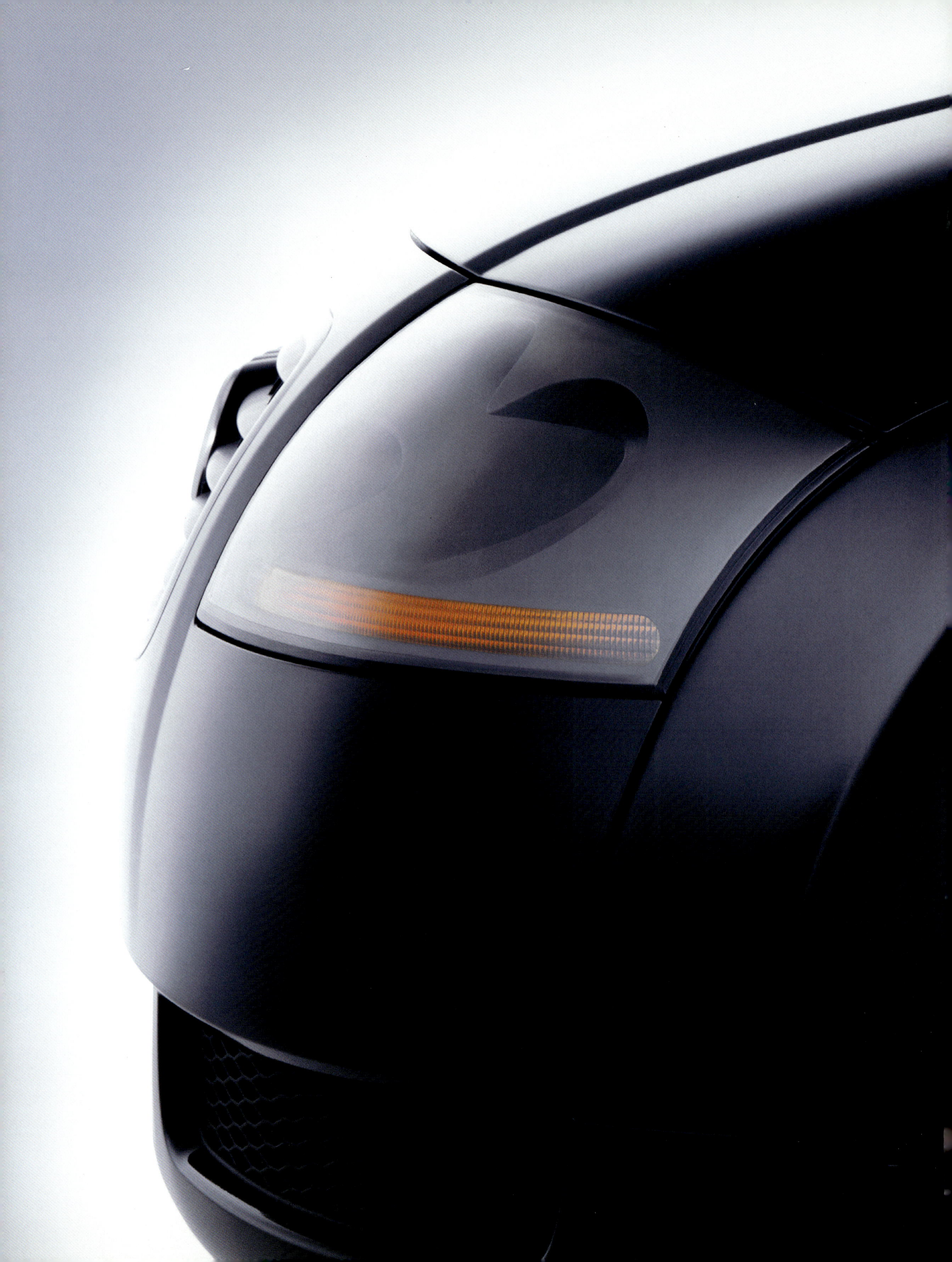

D E S I G N

297 MARKETING

①

297 COUPE

②

297 ROADSTER

{ 4 CYL 125 PS
4 CYL 150 PS TURBO
VR6 200 PS
FWD OR QUATTRO

③A

297 SPYDER
(39mm LOWER WINDSHIELD, SMALLER SIDEGLASS)

③B

297 SPYDER
W/HARDTOP (LOWDRAG)

{ 4 CYL 230 PS TURBO
VR6 230 PS
QUATTRO

▷ 3A + 3B WOULD BE SPECIALLY BUILT BY "AUDI SPORT"

Thomas 95©
MAR 7

Design

Design

In the Beginning was the Idea

by Jürgen Lewandowski

IN THE BEGINNING WAS THE WORD, or so the Bible tells us. For designers, a slightly modified version of this classic truth would seem to apply – the beginning of their work is the idea, the inspiration.

Ideas are what designers have in large quantities and what large companies and industrial groups then attempt to transform into reality. Every automobile manufacturer, after all, builds up its own model lines – and within relatively constant time cycles, these become technically and visually obsolescent and have to be modernised.

This process, admittedly, provides relatively little scope for genuinely new and highly unusual ideas, since these would have to be quite remarkably good before they would convert successfully into the tangible reality of the dealer's showroom.

If we take as a yardstick the degree of acceptance, the enthusiasm and the hymns of praise that were earned by the Audi TT Coupé at the German 'IAA' exhibition in Frankfurt in the autumn of 1995 and by the Roadster at the Tokyo Motor Show, it seems pretty certain that the idea behind these two designs actually deserves to be called a stroke of genius.

A small group of designers evidently came up with one of those rare "mega-ideas" that seldom see the light of day within a large company.

Not surprisingly, trade magazines such as *auto motor und sport* soon picked up the scent.

As early as April 1995 an article entitled "Attention Aluminium" enthused about a new aluminium-bodied roadster with four-wheel drive which was alleged to represent an "early glimpse of the future". With the aid of hindsight it may seem amusing to us that the Stuttgart-based magazine got the car's appearance quite wrong and sketched out a roadster with a roll hoop in the style of a Ferrari 250 LM, but the fact is that the authors were basically on the right track. The Ingolstadt automobile manufacturer's designers were indeed working on a new sports car.

In previous years, Audi had displayed not one but two highly impressive coupés: the first of these was the power-packed "Avus", with a 509 horsepower "W" pattern twelve-cylinder engine that would certainly have made it a tremendous performer, with a top speed of 340 kilometres an hour or more. It had a polished aluminium body that was interpreted as an act of homage to the Auto Union "Silver Arrow" racing cars of the nineteen-thirties.

The second was the quattro spyder, with a 174 horsepower engine, that captured potential buyers' imagination to such an extent that thousands of advance orders were received almost immediately.

Unfortunately, the quattro spyder failed to make it to production status because it was not built on an existing platform: a new chassis and running gear would have had to be developed as well as the new body. All the tooling for this would have made the car so expensive, even if it had been built in fairly large numbers, that it would probably never have been a commercial success.

It's difficult to believe - but tiny sketches such as these, produced within the Design department, can be the starting point for a totally new era. Their stark simplicity is none the less capable of changing our view of familiar objects.

"This car speaks German"

Confirmed by signature:
The TT's shape was finalised as early as May 23rd, 1994. This may well be the key to the TT's success: its shape was not subsequently modified, but managed to retain the spontaneity of the original creation throughout the development years.

As the dream of being able to purchase a quattro spyder waned, and disappointed customers wept into their handkerchiefs, the designers learned an unavoidable lesson: that there was indeed demand for an Audi sports car, but that it would have to be based on a series-production model in order to keep the price down to a sensible level.

"Our idea was simply to prove that a no-compromise car of character can be built on an economically viable basis", says Peter Schreyer today when recalling how the initial concept for the new car arose. "We knew perfectly well that we couldn't build a car capable of enhancing the company image if we economised at every possible opportunity – but we wanted to keep in touch with reality so that the cost controllers didn't destroy our dreams once again."

Independently of these considerations, development engineer Dr. Ulrich Hackenberg and his colleague Ralf-Gerhard Willner had presented the then Technical Director and subsequent President of the Board, Dr. Franz-Josef Paefgen, with a package drawing showing the potential for a shortened A3 chassis. "That was when things really took off", Paefgen recalls. "After that, Freeman Thomas was asked to make something out of it".

It was no surprise, therefore, when in May/June 1994 several of Freeman Thomas' initial roadster sketches appeared on the desk of design chief J. Mays. His sketches were considered so success-ful that he was asked to take the work home to his apartment and produce drawings of greater accuracy there.

It was not long, however – and this is where the unfortunate experience with the quattro spyder played its part – before Freeman Thomas was teamed with Ralf-Gerhard Willner, a pre-development engineer. The idea was for even the team's initial ideas to be based firmly on volume-production engineering, so that the difficulties associated with the launch of a brand-new car could be minimised.

What sets the TT (a name it only acquired later) apart from other cars in its category is the sheer pleasure of a shape that differs so much from the rest. In a later conversation, Freeman Thomas commented on the car's unique outlines with the words "This car speaks German!" By this, he certainly could not have meant "Teutonic" in any narrow sense of the term, since design studios are now located all round the globe and staffed by thoroughly international teams.

Ever since it introduced the quattro driveline, the fully galvanised body and the aluminium space frame (just a few of the company's technical innovations), Audi has clearly been a technology-led company. It was therefore essential for both the closed and open versions of the new sports car to be designs that first and foremost satisfied the domestic market's craving for technical perfection.

Design

ABSOLUT

▷ "ABSO[...]
EVERY[...]
AND E[...]
IN A[...]

▷ FORM
OVERALL DESIGN THEME IS OF TEUTONIC PURITY IN FORM. EVERY LINE AND FORM MUST BE JUSTIFIED BY ITS FUNCTION. VORSPRUNG DURCH TECHNIC

Thomas 94 ©

▷ SILLS SHAPED T[...]
REDUCE DRAG A[...]
AND MINIMIZE "ST[...]

...RM, SHAPE, FUNCTION,
...LL MUST COME TOGETHER
"ABSOLUT" RESULT.

▸ REAR LAMPS W/ NEON
TURN SIGNAL

PURE

▸ EXHAUST PIPES FACING
DOWNWARD, PERFORATED
ALUMINIUM HEAT SHIELD

COUPE

▸ LOW-DRAG CABIN

FORM

▸ "MATURE"
DESIGN SHOULD FEEL
"GROWN-UP." ALL AGE
GROUPS, MEN & WOMEN
SHOULD FEEL
LIKE "WEAR-
ING" THIS
COUPE.

▸ COUPE SHOULD FEEL
SERIOUS AND NOT
CHILDISH.

MATURE

"SCHLAG"

The fascination of innovative engineering

Hundreds of sketches are made as part of the process of arriving at the final form - all with one single aim in mind: to hone and polish a brilliant idea until an attractive automobile materialises.

As the first rapid sketches slowly took shape and an entirely individual outline began to appear, those involved in the process were glad to see that the new car's silhouette possessed just the mixture of features loaned from the past and visionary glimpses of the future that is typical of every effective design capable of making history.

The first drawings had soon given rise to the desire not only to realise the constantly fascinating roadster concept but also to produce a coupé. One of the reasons for this decision was the fact that there was no current coupé on the market with "designer quality", and that such an additional model version would also have a beneficial effect on the economic picture.

In this way, the open and closed models began to take shape in parallel, both with a number of felicitous visual references to the styles of earlier years, in particular the short wheelbase, compact body dimensions and sporting proportions.

Not that the nostalgic aspects of the design should be over-emphasised: the world has changed a lot in recent decades, and the "dream cars" of the 1960s and 1970s with their more ample proportions, their chromium plate and their power and sound tended to be well out of most people's reach. For the creators of the new Coupé and Roadster, sheer speed and driving pleasure were clearly important, but other factors were too.

As an emphatically sporting product from a company with a high reputation for advanced automobile technology, the new cars had the task of communicating other messages too — the fascination exerted by technical innovation, a high level of environmental acceptability and of course the safety and quality associated with a marque that had acquired a special place in automobile manufacturing in recent years on the basis of precisely these characteristics.

The remarkable thing about the TT is that its blend of futuristic design and the evident delight in classic details such as the 1930-ish fuel filler cap, the affectionately designed dash panel or the ventilation outlets which could have come straight from the drawing board of a member of the famous "Bauhaus", although difficult to grow accustomed to initially, soon become almost self-evident to the onlooker. In due course one is ready to concede that a coupé from Audi simply has to look like this.

So it was that a small team consisting of Freeman Thomas, Ralf-Gerhard Willner and two modellers from Manfred Schotzer's team moved into a small studio away from the factory, in a rented building close to Ingolstadt. It was here within the next two months that the initial quarter-scale model took shape. It is important to remember in this context that from the first few weeks on the coupé and the roadster were developed in parallel: "The two versions had the same priority. Neither of them was given preference", says Thomas.

Once a number of quarter-scale models had been produced, they were presented to Group Chairman Ferdinand Piëch. "I like it!" was his brief comment.

The design study – from which the TT was later to develop – undoubtedly represents one of those rare moments when a small group of designers and engineers has the chance to create a product in which the joy of creativity is uppermost. "The TT is the absolute opposite of what is commonly referred to as a car designed by a committee" explained Peter Schreyer, Head of Audi Design, during the demonstration drives in Italy in the summer of 1998. "It's not the result of a thousand compromises. It's the realisation of a vision. It was created by a small, 'conspiratorial' group of enthusiasts whose work was based on three main characteristics: passion, love of detail and consistency".

Freeman Thomas – alleged by his colleagues to be more German than any German – was never at a loss for a suitable word to describe how he saw the new car: "Absolute! We wanted an 'absolute' shape, the same as a Leica camera, for instance, or a 'Bauhaus' design."

Thomas was a strong believer in the notion that Audi, as a German automobile company, could define itself most effectively by means of classic visual quotations from the 'Bauhaus' period, when strict forms were the order of the day and form was most definitely expected to follow function. But the results had to be scrutinised constantly to see whether the function itself was sensible. Should it be concentrated to an even greater extent? Was the temptation to indulge in superficial decoration being resisted? Was the technical aspect clearly taking precedence over all others?

The cool formal language of this kind of industrial design does not necessarily rule out an emotional reaction. Peter Schreyer comments on the difficult area of tension between form and response by saying "Function always includes emotional and sporting character."

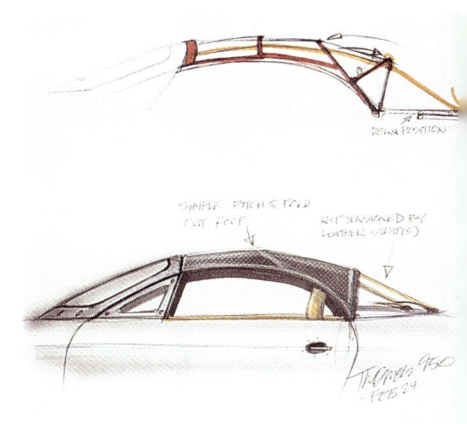

Design

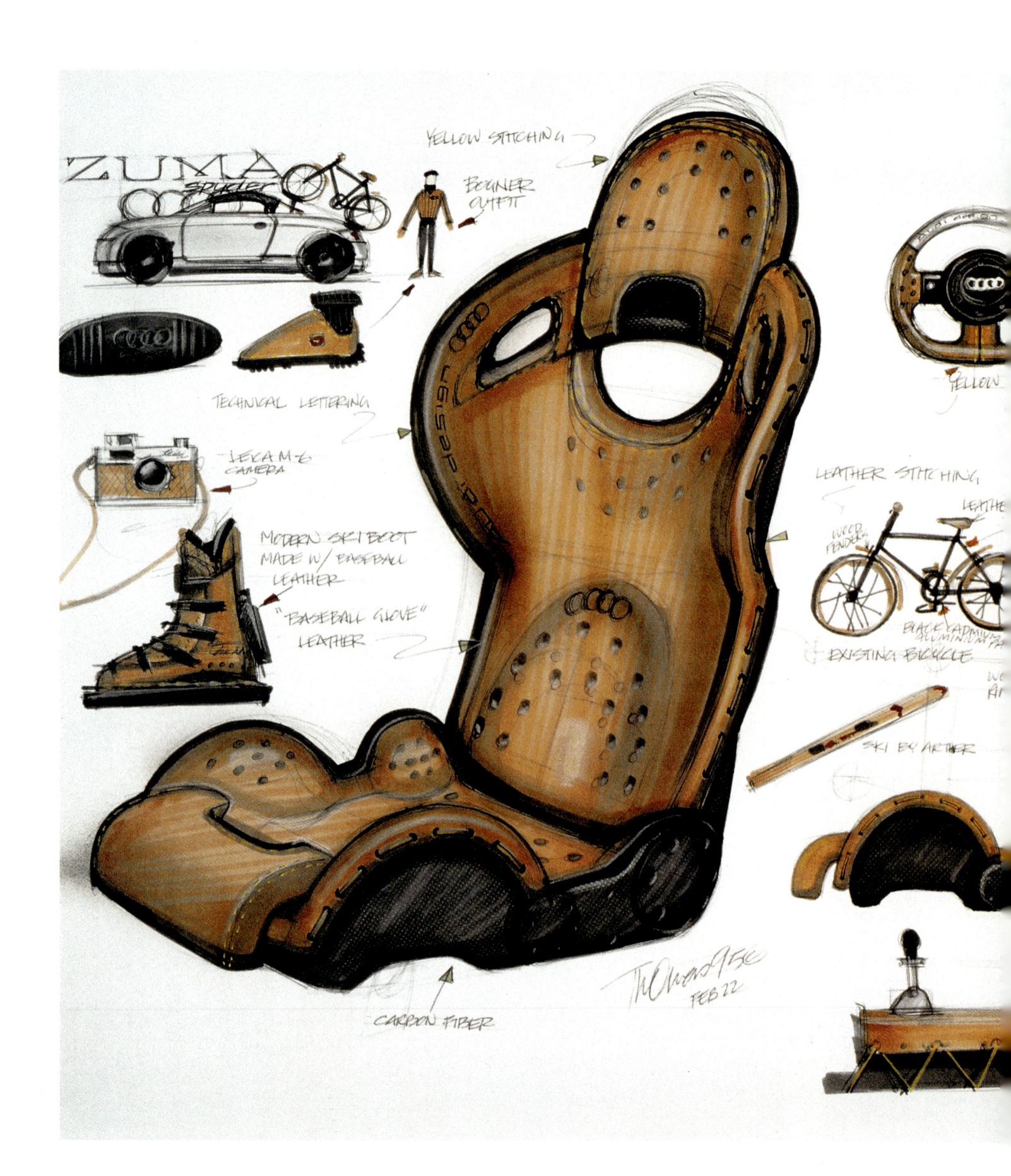

Design

A sports car for the purist

For Schreyer, who as Head of Audi Design was naturally up-to-date on the activities of the small but dedicated TT design team, its members' unceasing urge to examine the validity of every single pencil line, every technical suggestion and every design or equipment detail was almost manic in character: "We wanted to build a pure sports car, and we dedicated ourselves wholeheartedly to achieving a new kind of unity between technical features and driving pleasure."

Even during the initial discussions between the Design and Technical Development departments, it quickly became clear that the A3 was eminently suitable as a technical foundation for the TT – and it was on this basis that the team set to work refining the outlines of the body still further.

Having made this technical decision, further refinement of the new car's outlines was able to go ahead.

In the weeks that followed, the first informal sketches were steadily revised until the final shape began to materialise. The use of a transverse front-mounted engine clearly invited the designers to adopt a cab-forward layout, with a short nose section and the passenger area starting a relatively long way towards the front. Freeman Thomas on this decision: "We didn't want to suggest a long roadster nose section by some trick or other, but to take the transverse engine layout as it stood and build a super coupé on that basis."

'Absolute' -
this was the word used to check the validity of every body line, every screw head, every shape on the entire car.
This drawing shows how many suggestions were taken up and put into effect.

A commitment to circular forms

Peter Schreyer sees the TT design as "to a large extent led by the wheels, first of all because of the almost geometrical shape of the wheel arches and the way they stand out from the body, but also because of the way the shoulder line follows the front and rear wheel arch cutouts and thus maintains close contact with the wheels. It is this design aspect above all that gives the TT such an exceptionally compact appearance."

Almost eight weeks had by now elapsed – but in this short time the TT had taken shape, and the next step was for the interior to be designed in a similarly distinctive formal idiom. This task was entrusted to Romulus Rost, who joined the still small team in August.

Rost, a Romanian by birth, was delighted by the quarter-scale model when he first saw it in the late summer: "It was an overwhelming shape, so clear and so simple, but with a totally unique character.

Such a remarkable model as this deserved an equally special interior. Even at that early stage it exuded a spirit all its own."

Interestingly enough, although speaking in German, Rost makes use of the English word "spirit" in this context.

In order to reflect on ways and means of creating an interior that would do justice to this car's outward appearance, Rost visited the American Audi Design Studio in Simi Valley for a few months in September 1994, and was there able to work on a seat buck for the new car and allow his initial ideas to mature in a calm, peaceful atmosphere.

Shortly before Christmas he flew back with a large pile of full-scale drawings, only to have those who examined them ask the provocative question: "Hasn't the interior come out a bit too simple?"

Rost was half expecting this question; he had used his spell in America to look more closely at ways of incorporating aluminium into the car's interior. The result proved to be an extremely "purist" design which, in his words, "confronts the onlooker systematically with a taut, compact dash panel. Its bold, arc-shaped instrument hood with its circular dials – in a layout that recalls the company's four-ring emblem – follows the curve of the steering wheel rim in a most logical way. The instruments themselves have exceptionally clear graphics, aimed at reducing the visual effect to an honest minimum."

Inside the car, there are many further references to the circle as a basic design element. All the details – air outlets, switches, gear lever gate and the shape of the centre console – are matched together most carefully. It is this stylistic harmony between interior and exterior which has made the TT what its designers call an 'absolute' sports car.

Romulus Rost was joined by Winfried Rückheim in the task of interpreting the designer's inspiration in terms of practical reality. The overriding challenge facing their work was to achieve a harmonious association between the design itself and the material, aluminium, which is given such a prominent role to play in it.

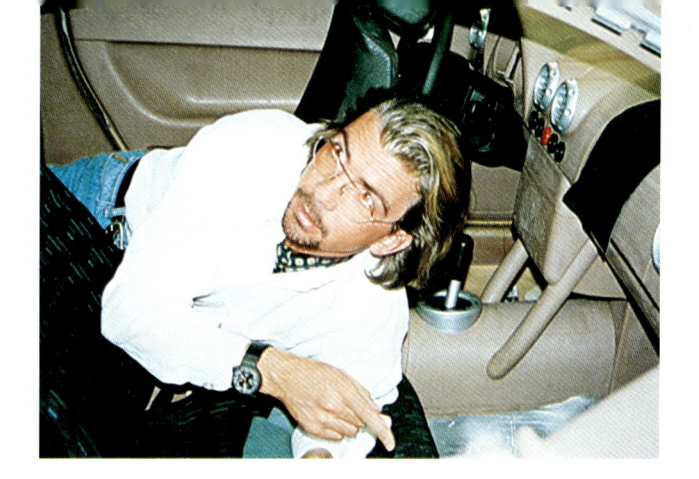

"It's important for the observer to see that human beings have undertaken this work."
Romulus Rost

What does Romulus Rost have to say on this subject? "Everyone knows that Audi is closely involved with this material – for us, aluminium has had a contribution to make towards improving both economic and ecological conditions that didn't just start when the A8 was introduced. We naturally wanted the TT to take its place in this pattern of development. My task was therefore to make use of aluminium as an interior design element as well."

This was aided by the fact that aluminium is an "honest, high-class material with a sporting aura that matches the TT perfectly. It was important for us to use genuine aluminium at appropriate points inside the car, and not to content ourselves with plastic coated to look like metal."

In his initial designs, Rost was determined to achieve one thing in particular: for the observer to develop an immediate liking for the car.

"I wanted him or her to feel the urge to touch it! The sense of touch is very important indeed, but the materials must also be well-chosen and the workmanship must exhibit a convincing love of detail. It's also essential for the onlooker to gain the impression that real live human beings have been at work here – the leather has to smell like leather, the seams have to reveal that they were sewn by hand."

As the weeks and months passed, the car's body and interior design were continually refined, though always subject to the right answer being given to the question: "Is it still an 'absolute' design?"

Peter Schreyer has this to say: "This term 'absolute' seemed to crop up all the time during the draft design phase. We were determined that the TT should be an 'absolute' design in its overall outline, its joint and panel lines, in fact everything. Even the smallest sketches had to conform to this principle. Are the ventilation outlets 'absolute' enough? Is that an 'absolute' headlight? If anything fell short of this definition, we threw it out and started again. You can imagine the sheer attention to detail that went into even the smallest aspects of the design, and the way we checked all the materials for authenticity: if it looks like aluminium, then it has to be made of aluminium – for instance the fuel filler cap or the air vents inside the car."

During its search for the 'absolute', the studio team worked to a constant background of music by Frank Zappa, Jimi Hendrix and Miles Davis.
What influence this may have had is impossible to establish now, but it surely contributed in some way to the TT's individuality.

In March 1995 the first full-scale models of the exterior and interior were ready, in this case still in clay, and representing the Coupé. Later a mould was made, the roof removed and the first full-size representation of the Roadster completed.

Design

Now all doubts were dispelled: the shape was a success. The team had created what was fundamentally a simple basic form, with generous curved outlines and a simple, clearly defined pattern of panel and joint lines.

In addition to the more striking design elements such as the headlights and other lights or the shield-shaped rear window, the TT's appearance is above all influenced by the circle – a graphic element that is perfect in itself.

Peter Schreyer comments: "The circle is a symbol of our striving for the absolute, and is featured at various points both inside and outside the car. The fuel filler cap, for example, which is not normally given an prominence, is emphasised here as a technical and sporting element. With its brushed aluminium finish, it is a jewel-like decorative feature of the body."

At the end of 1994 the current Audi chief executive Franz-Josef Paefgen suggested that instead of the coupé body with a single side window, a version with two side windows should be investigated. The first models confirmed that this version certainly made the interior of the car lighter and more pleasant, so that although the single-window version was shown at the German 'IAA' in Frankfurt, the Coupé was prepared for production with the larger window area.

"We were naturally assuming that the TT would sooner or later go into volume production, and this was a powerful source of motivation for the team," recalls Dr. Ulrich Hackenberg today when looking back at the period between the autumn of 1994 and the car's first appearance twelve months later in Frankfurt. "The emotional effect varies according to whether you're working on an unrealistic show car or a 'dream car' that's nonetheless likely to reach the dealer's showroom in due course."

We ought to get to know Ulrich Hackenberg more closely: as Project Coordinator, it was his task to organise the designers and technicians into an operational team after the board of management had given the project its go-ahead, and to bring some semblance of order and feasibility to their widely disparate ideas and concepts.

There was certainly any number of questions still to be answered. Apart from those directly concerned with design, the big one was clearly the technical basis to be used for the two prototypes. First of all, various parameters had to be defined, for example which platform would be suitable for the new Coupé and the planned Roadster?

Peter Schreyer again: "We constantly asked ourselves: what technical resources do we have at our disposal that suit our purpose? And apart from that, what can we justify financially?"

Design

A gem of an exterior

The next question was: what engines should be installed under the aluminium bonnet? For the TT design study, the choice fell on the 110 kW (150 bhp) 1.8-litre four-cylinder turbocharged unit from the A4, with five valves per cylinder. Since the Coupé weighed only 1,220 kilograms, this engine was able to propel it to an estimated top speed of 225 km/h.

For a company that had gained such a high reputation with its *quattro* four-wheel drive, such figures were perhaps not of prime importance, and in any case, everyone concerned was aware of the fact that they were still hypothetical – reality was to turn out differently.

Another aspect of the TT project was equally fascinating: the urge to save weight, in other words the art of reducing the design to essentials but not sacrificing anything needed to ensure driving pleasure.

The design study therefore had a load-bearing steel body structure, but with all the attached panels and doors, the large luggage compartment lid and the bonnet made of aluminium. At a relatively early stage it was also decided to equip the TT design study with rear seats that would accommodate adult passengers in comfort for a short distance.

A further decision was also taken: to use pre-production parts for most of the two prototypes' components, after subjecting them to the necessary fine tuning.

Parallel to the Coupé, work was of course started on determining the TT Roadster's technical specification. It was to be powered by a 154 kW (210 bhp) version of the 1.8-litre four-cylinder engine, giving it a top speed of 240 km/h and enabling it to accelerate from 0 to 100 km/h in about six seconds.

After the Coupé and the Roadster had been inspected once more and approved by the company's board of management, Freeman Thomas and Romulus Rost took themselves off to Italy, where the Italdesign company had been commissioned to build the two prototypes for the Frankfurt and Tokyo Motor Shows in its hermetically sealed workshop in Moncalieri, near Turin. The two cars were assembled there at a hectic place, but were at least free from the unwanted attentions of photographers who specialise in sneak previews of forthcoming models.

Even the smallest detail sketch was expected to satisfy the all-embracing demand for the 'absolute'. If not, it was mercilessly rejected.

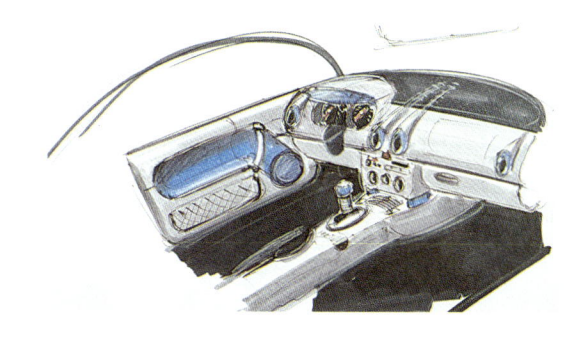

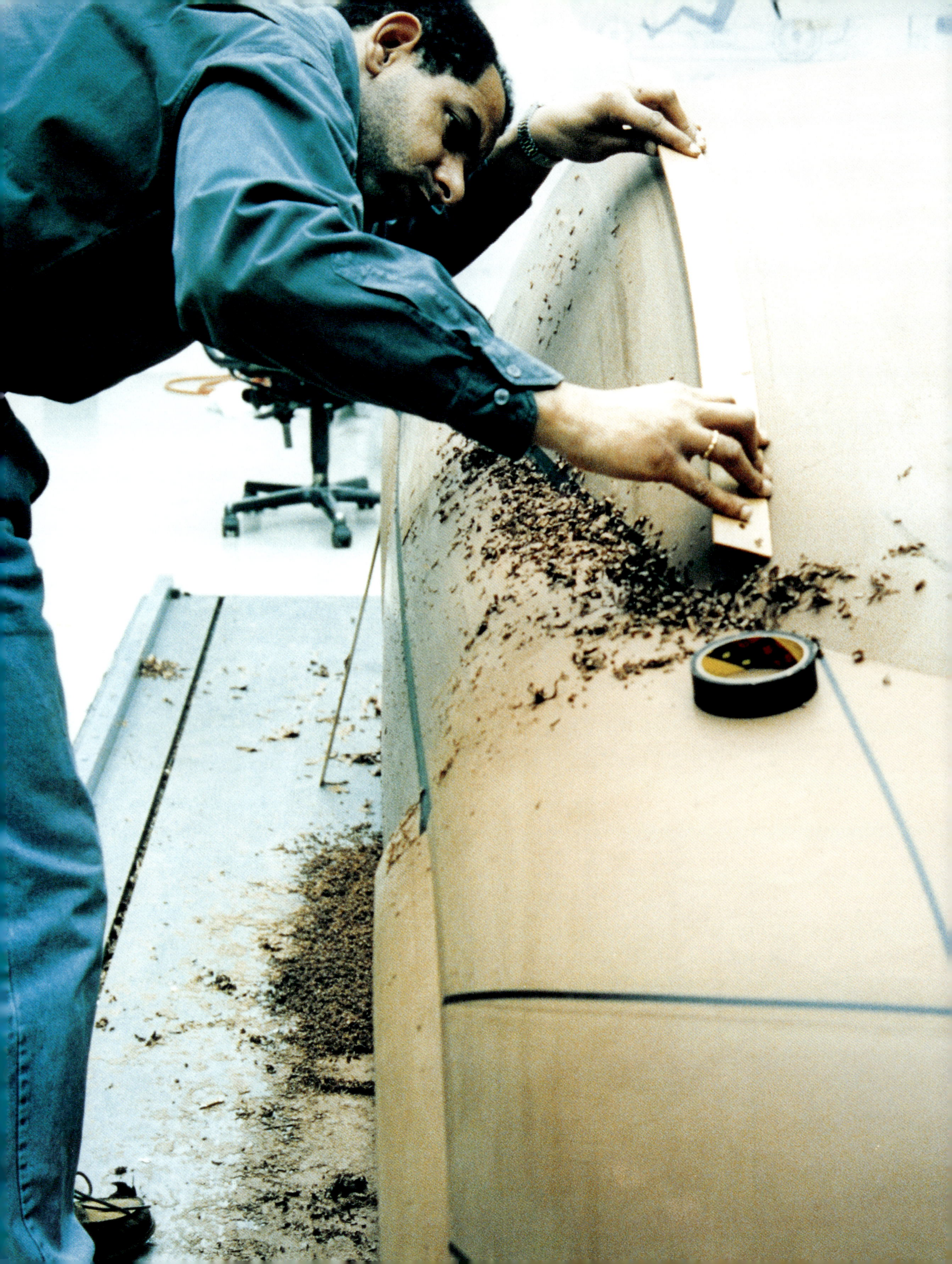

A definite "No"!

Italdesign was chosen not only because it had already built numerous prototypes for the Volkswagen Group, but also because its proprietor, Giorgetto Giugiaro and his craftsmen (who surely ought to be described as artists) were noted for their ability to keep a secret. They have proved capable of conjuring up a roadgoing prototype within a few weeks, and as soon as the two designers from Ingolstadt arrived they began to work their way through the various drawings and models supplied to them and set about constructing the two cars that were destined to amaze motoring journalists and the general public alike in September and November of that year.

The two cars were built in conditions of the most remarkable secrecy: although Giugiaro naturally knew that his staff were working on his contract from Audi in their hermetically sealed building, he wasn't even allowed through his own gates to see the results until permission had been obtained from Audi in Ingolstadt! His reaction? Romulus Rost recalls: "He was delighted! He walked all round the cars, taking plenty of time over it, and studied their shape and proportions at length before declaring that the design was perfect. We asked him what we ought to change, but he declared firmly that there simply wasn't anything that needed improving."

The men from Italdesign built the two TT prototypes in the fantastically short time of only four months, starting with the Coupé but with work on the Roadster proceeding in parallel; the second car too was finished by the last week in August. To commemorate the occasion, Freeman Thomas and Romulus Rost treated themselves to a cigar on their last evening in Turin – a Romeo y Julieta Nr. 3, the wrapper of which they signed, dated and placed ceremonially in the car's roll hoop before this was finally welded into place.

A few days before the German Motor Show was due to open its doors, the Coupé was delivered to the Ingolstadt factory, carefully checked and a few teething troubles eliminated: the passenger's door, for instance, refused to open and certain areas of the paintwork had to be touched in.

Then it was time for a press photo session with Peter Vann late in the afternoon, with the light fading rapidly and heavy rain falling. When this was finally over, one of the headlights was found to be leaking slightly and had to be repaired. At long last, the car was despatched to Frankfurt for its world première – but on arrival a few more unwelcome surprises were in store: neither of the electric windows was working, and technicians from Italdesign had to be flown up urgently from Milan to check through the electrical system before the electric motors could be coaxed into doing their work.

By then it was four in the morning before the big show – a very brief night's rest followed for all concerned.

It's never less than fascinating to watch the modellers at work: from a handful of sketches and plans, they create a three-dimensional model and transform an idea into material form.

While the TT took shape in Italdesign's workshops in Moncalieri, the designers in Ingolstadt used their computers to examine every possible TT version from 'purist' Roadster to out-and-out competition car, though without any intention of actually preparing such versions for production.

The reaction from the public, the media and other Design Department colleagues (who had never seen the TT until that very moment) was uniformly positive. The TT had been expected to give rise to divided opinions, but there was scarcely a voice raised in criticism, and those who had initially found its outlines too stark changed their mind in the weeks and months that followed, and became the most enthusiastic admirers of the two design studies.

Writing in *auto motor und sport* in February 1996 after attending a photo session in California with the photographer Wolfgang Drehsen, Clauspeter Becker declared: "Our attitude to the Audi TT and TTS started out as a professionally cool one. The restrained presentation of the Coupé on a separate section of the Audi stand at the 'IAA' had failed to arouse any great enthusiasm in either of us. And the 'grey' Roadster displays under equally grey light in Tokyo and Detroit didn't exactly turn us on either.

But after a day that the airline had artificially prolonged by nine hours, there came an 'encounter of the second kind': the Coupé arrived on its low-loader and was immediately caught by the magical light of a sunset on the Pacific Coast. That was when we ceased to be indifferent to this car. We could see how seductive it would be and accepted it as a clear response to what the future of the coupé should be."

The Austrian writer David Staretz can also be quoted here: "It's just amazing how good the results can be if you simply leave off everything unnecessary and emphasise the essentials. The evidently close cooperation between the technical people and the designers is particularly rewarding in certain areas: the neon-tube strip flashers (which unfortunately are not intended for series production), the frameless side windows with their automatic lowering action as the doors are opened and closed, the semi-recessed wipers with their trapezoidal action for an ideal wiped area and the brilliantly simple design inside the engine compartment. Every tangle of minor components and wiring has been concealed behind a black grid, with only the cylinder head, the various fillers and the dipstick projecting above it."

Enthusiasm knew no bounds, and the logical question was how soon the TT would be seen in the dealers' showrooms. By September 1995, just about every major publication had joined in the call for this car to be produced as soon as possible. Although the response on the part of the press and visitors to the show had more or less convinced Audi's board of management that series production would be a good thing, there was still no official announcement to that effect from Ingolstadt. Only a few people in the know were aware that the TT Coupé was to be followed seven weeks later by an open-topped design study, the TTS. The company wanted to await the public's reaction to both prototypes before reaching its final decision.

Discreetly under wraps

Design

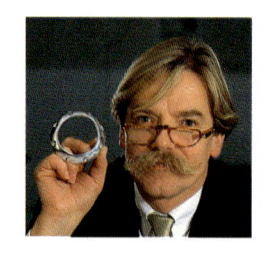

The project team:
Hayko Mayer,
Holger Baumann,
Martin Götze,
Dirk Obenhoff
(standing at left,
from left to right);
Manfred Limmer
(seated at left);
Peter Heine,
Wilhelm Straub,
Thomas Zwicknagl,
Rainer-Andreas Thomas,
Claus Haverkamp,
Lorenz Forster,
Helmut Kohl
(standing at right,
left to right);
Axel Bienhaus,
Albert Liebhart
(seated at right,
left to right).

Not that the verdict was ever in serious doubt: Stefan Härdl, for instance, was approached while the 'IAA' was still in progress and asked whether he would be prepared to undertake technical coordination for the TT – a most tempting task which this graduate engineer was more than willing to accept.

At that time the task of developing a series-production TT had only been defined in one, admittedly important, respect: it was to have a clearly defined budget.

"The workers at Italdesign had toiled day and night to finish our cars, even during the sacred Italian holiday months of August," Peter Schreyer recalls. "To be honest, building them was none of those unsung acts of industrial heroism that takes place very discreetly, regardless of what the carefully negotiated wage and working-hours agreements may call for." The TT Roadster (still known as the TTS, although this designation was to be discarded on series-production cars) was finished on time, but many an extra shift, including nights, had to be worked.

The team came up with a different idea for the TTS interior, Peter Schreyer remembers. "Someone suggested the baseball glove as a source of inspiration during one of our brainstorming sessions. We all felt that this type of game, with its vigorous ball-throwing and catching, was a good starting point. We were fascinated by the quality of the leather and the powerful visual effect of the cross-stitching on the catcher's glove."

Romulus Rost thereupon designed the Roadster's leather seats in the classic rust-coloured leather with the authentic cross-stitching that suggests America's national sport and the big gloves worn by baseball catchers. In most other respects, the Roadster was very similar to the Coupé, though the silver paint finish seen at the 'IAA' had given way to a dark grey decor with the rust-red "baseball" upholstery mentioned above on the open car. There was also a small air outlet between the front wheel arch and the door.

The remarkably 'absolute' shape had lost nothing, apart from the roof, which itself had been removed, as the designers might well have said, in a thoroughly 'absolute' way.

Writing in *Autofocus*, David Staretz described the development process in the following terms: "The story so far: Audi has achieved a 'tour de force' and reestablished the classic Porsche mental approach. A small, carefully cocooned team of designers and technical people was given this commission, and within a year it was there on the platform for everyone to see: THE THING, the 'ugly TT', a distillation of pure automobile without a single crack

Design

From understatement to statement

between the molecules – an instant classic at the 'IAA'. Followed by Tokyo: an even more powerful concentrate, closer still to the pure automobile concept. Seldom have bare necessities been packaged in such eye-catching form.

People who came face to face with this car tended to go home in possession of an entirely new thought: beautiful and ugly are often rather desperate definitions. This particular vehicle is applied art that goes beyond the scope of such terms and into the region of power design, instinctive motoring, cocooning, young lovers and anything else that belongs there. But certainly not anything we care to introduce arbitrarily.

One solitary rule still had to be verified: what's good in closed form is even better when open. In all fairness, we should remember that the convertible concept grew up together with the design study as a whole, and that for a while the open version actually seemed as if it would be the TT first. The TTS sings the same lyrics in a topless version, and leaves the interpretation to us.

The problem is quite simple: how to live without a beautiful neck. The answer was to expose the tendons, in the form of two retaining straps that tension the somewhat existential soft top (which is not much more than an umbrella over the occupants' heads) toward the rear. Given proper convertible-type weather, the two steel roll-over hoops sparkle in the sun and also perform their serious task of protecting our heads.

Their visual character ties in well with the 'war chariot' effect of the big, aluminium spoked 18-inch wheels and the closed visor suggested by the radiator grille."

Both prototypes certainly had a polarising effect. "This was even true inside Audi itself", says Peter Schreyer, "but the more often those in the secret got to see the car, the more enthusiastic they became. As time went on, all of them began to insist that both versions should go into production."

As we have already implied, Audi had been a technology-led company for some years now. Its design chief formulated this somewhat differently in conversation: "For a long time the cars we built were intended to suggest understatement. Now things have changed. One of my colleagues put it this way: 'We've progressed from understatement to statement'. I like that. I've often asked myself exactly how it came about – it must have something to do with the proportions, with the way the wheels are seen to carry the body: a relatively long way forward, and very central. This is a design feature that's now shared by all Audis, but you can see it particularly well on the TT."

"This is how our cars acquire their individuality, their well-balanced character but at the same time this sense of thrusting forwards. Other important design features are the high sides and comparatively low window height. This gives the occupants a feeling of security and safety – as well as looking powerful and sporting from the onlooker's point of view."

Peter Schreyer, Audi's Design chief (below):
"This car not only looks as if it's well made technically - it is!"

Pictures above, from left to right: Harry Bechtel, Technical/Interior Design Manager, Ulrike Dust, Color & Trim Manager, Jürgen Schröder, Interior Design, Torsten Wenzel, Exterior Design, Barbara Krömeke, Color & Trim, Frank Gruner, Exterior Design

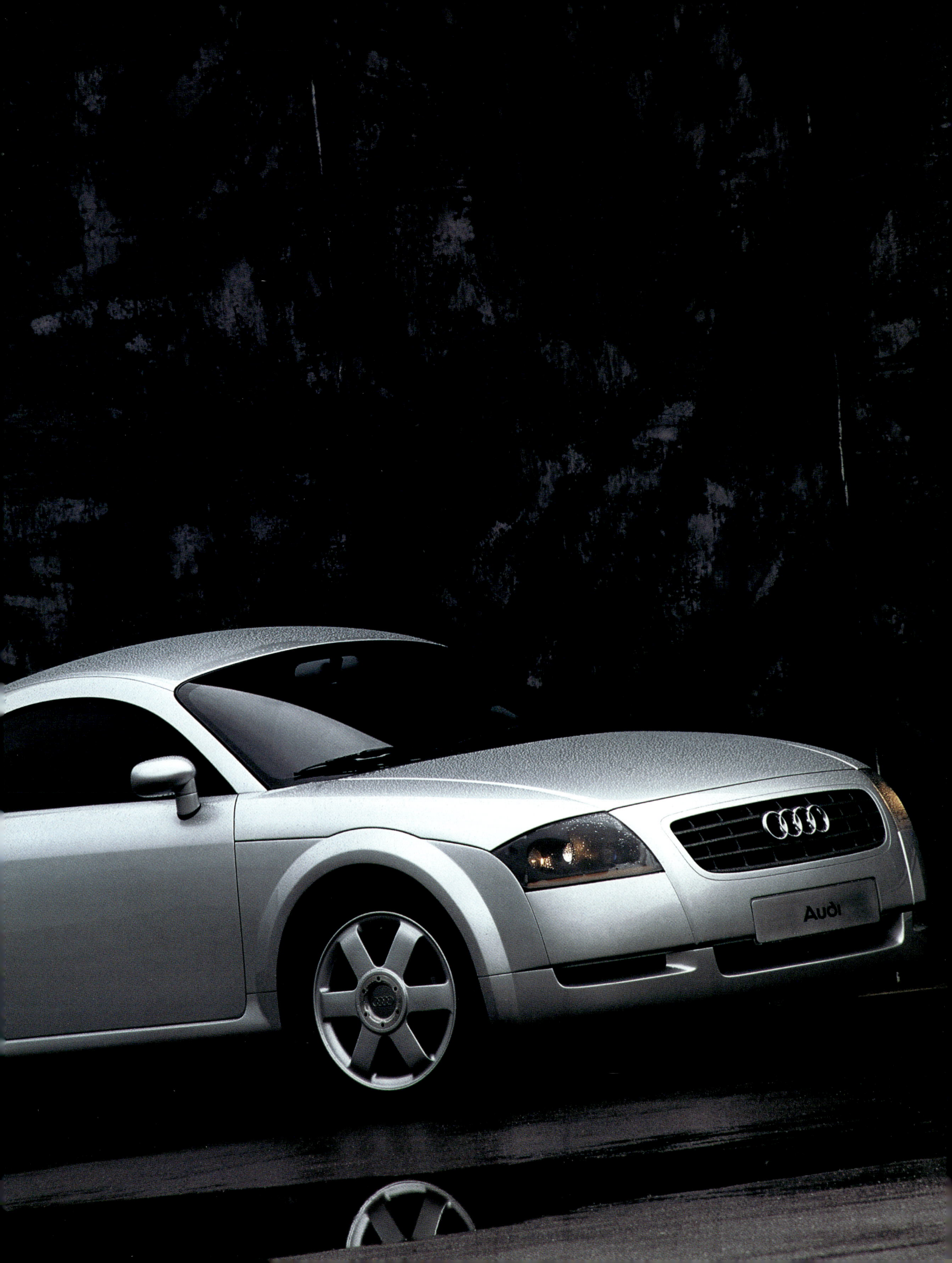
Audi

In this car, everyone looks good

It was probably a mixture of many individual characteristics that led to the TT and its open-topped sister-model being accepted so whole-heartedly by so many sports-car enthusiasts: a combination of the pure, uncluttered styling and the absence of any trivial design 'gimmicks'.

The car is 'of a piece' in this respect, so that David Staretz, for instance, suspects that "it clearly wasn't worked on and monkeyed about with for the usual five or six years needed to develop a new car. Smaller cells grow faster and more actively, maybe in a single year, and this makes them up-to-date and also more unified in their concept."

This is how the TT was able to develop the unusual design philosophy that Freeman Thomas and Romulus Rost summed up at the presentation in October 1995: "This car not only looks streamlined – it is.

This car not only looks well made technically – it is! It looks fast – it is fast. But it isn't an aggressive car. It merely declares itself to be highly capable in a number of ways. It doesn't say 'Out of the way, here I come!' It's a car in which anyone looks good: women, men, the young and the old. From students to top managers – everyone looks their best in this car." This conclusion led to the most important decision of all being made, the board of management having been so impressed by the reaction to the TT in Frankfurt as to have no option but to consider making it.

The TTS caused an equal furore in Tokyo and meant that by October 1995 instructions had been issued to develop both cars to series-production readiness.

The TT is evidence that close cooperation between Engineering and Design can achieve quite outstanding results - such as those that helped to give the TT its individuality.

The TT just had to go into series production

With its 'baseball glove' seats, *brilliantly simple wheel rims and deceptively simple dash panel, the TT Roadster design study became a favourite with the public – what alternative did Audi have but to build it?*

This decision was not allowed to leak out immediately – indeed it was some months before the management in Ingolstadt ceased to deny any intention of producing the Coupé and Roadster in volume. Attentive observers would have detected the answer back in October 1995, at the Audi press conference in Tokyo, when both prototypes were positioned (for the first and last time) on a single platform, and VW chief executive Ferdinand Piëch was heard to say proudly: "A few more years may elapse before you see both these design studies in the same place again."

In other words, he was well aware that one fine day we *would* see them together again.

Design

T E C H N

I   C   A   L

Dimensions Audi TT Roadster

The TT: classic, visionary

Making the car mobile

By Jürgen Lewandowski

THE MAJOR MOTOR SHOWS HAVE SOMETHING MAGICAL ABOUT THEM – the sheer numbers of new cars on display take one's breath away, the design engineers' skills in coming up with new technical methods and devices never cease to amaze, and then there are the stylists! Although most of us know by now what a car consists of, they constantly succeed in giving this basically mundane object new shapes and colours and thus obliging us to see it in a new light. This is where trends are born and forms presented that will determine our visual response to the automobile in the years to come, possibly for a decade or more.

It was at just such an international motor show that the TT captured the public's attention for the first time. At the 1995 "IAA" in Frankfurt, Germany, a familiar theme was re-interpreted to give a totally new answer to the question *"How do I stimulate the emotions with a coupé?"* For every visitor and the numerous expert automobile industry observers who attended this show, the answer was obvious: the Audi TT had ushered in a new chapter in the history of car design. The wedge outline was obliged to make way for newer, more curvaceous, more organic forms. Many fans began to ask themselves whether a sports car had to bristle with spoilers merely in order to justify the name.

Later, Audi chief executive Franz-Josef Paefgen was heard to comment: "The new model's message is clearly defined by two terms: classic and visionary. Associations with sports cars of the 1950s are deliberate, and the letters TT stand for tradition and technology."

Undeniably though, they also stand for the classic Tourist Trophy race, held for the first time on the Isle of Man in 1905. This was a most welcome coincidence, and one that gave tradition and technology a desirable motorsport background. To quote the press release issued for the TT's presentation in Gubbio, Italy, in September 1998:

"The name chosen for this car does justice to its sporting character and emphasises the special claims made for it. In addition, TT is a short, striking and straight-down-the-line name – as purist in style as the TT itself."

From the moment of its conception the TT was guided along ist way by engineers who backed the stylists' whims with convincing technical solutions, and played their part in taming design creativity only to the extent needed to make it suitable for modern high-volume production methods. The engineers evolved the "map-square" principle for both the interior and exterior of the new car. Under the leadership of Ralf-Gerhard Willner, they divided it up into reference sections which had to be confirmed in each case as technically feasible. In this way the two prototypes were readied for the Frankfurt and Tokyo motor shows; they could be driven, though they were naturally still a long way from series-production maturity.

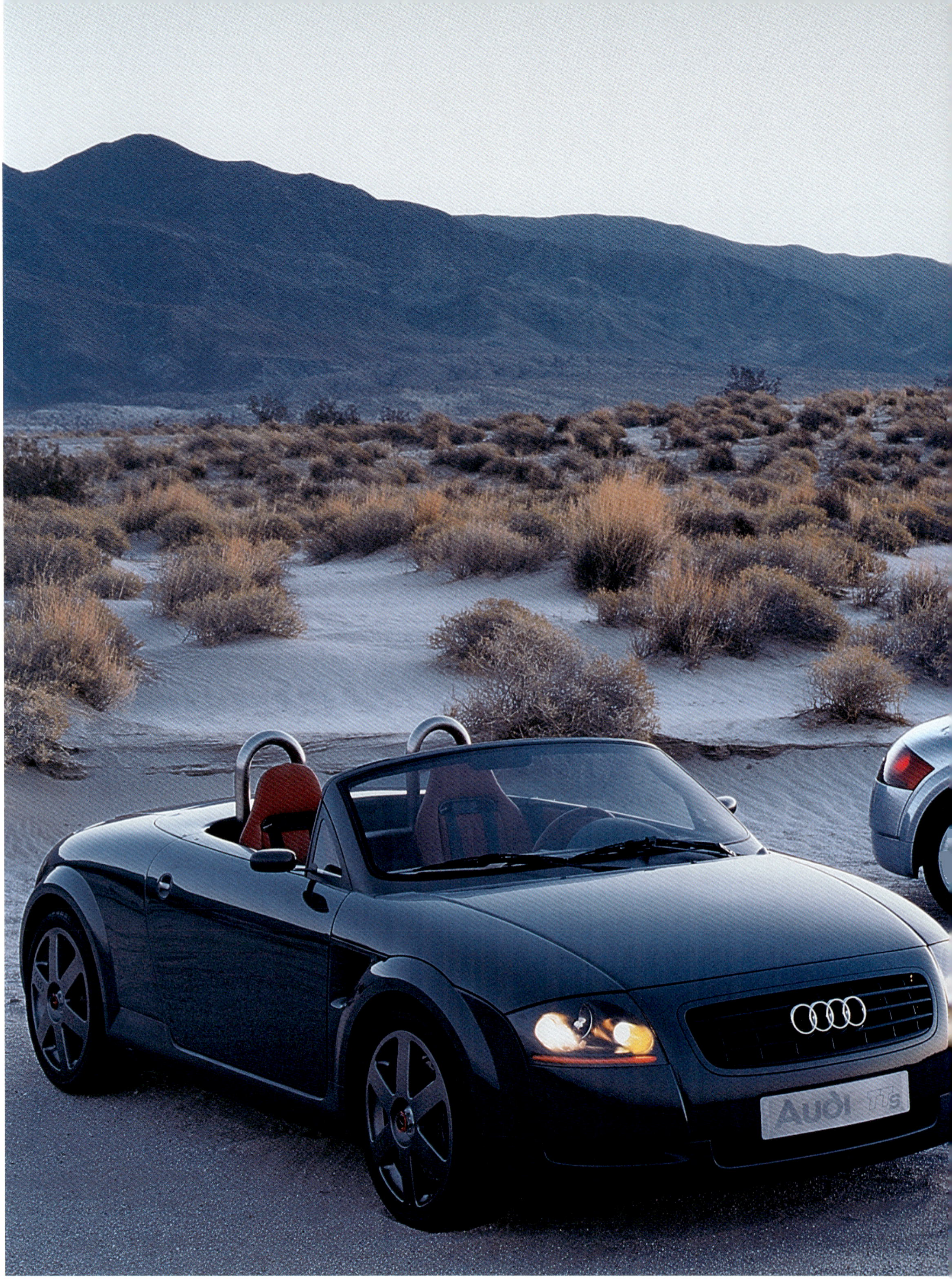
Audi TTS

Two of a kind – *a particularly valuable kind. With its TT Coupé and TT Roadster, Audi launched two sports cars that made design history from the very day of their announcement onwards. Within a very short time, these two models were to become modern classics.*

Technical

The TT's unmistakable character

"Of course they were both in roadgoing condition", Willner recalls. "But don't forget that they were more or less priceless one-off prototypes, and our engineers had planned for them to have various components that were still under development and only existed on the computer screen. In other words, some of the hardware was still missing."

Before the first test drives could be offered to the press and volume production could get under way, the teams led by Peter Schreyer and Stefan Härdl had many months, not to say years, of hard work ahead of them, including many nights without the recommended number of hours of sleep.

Stefan Härdl joined the design team in due course as its new project coordination manager.

Thanks to the work already done, he was able to remove several basic questions from the agenda almost immediately. The first chassis was derived from an initial version of the A platform which had been developed in Wolfsburg for use in the Golf IV and the Audi A3. The front wheels were to have McPherson suspension, the rear wheels a combined trailing arm and double wishbone layout with separate spring and shock absorber mountings. When it came to the engines, the decision was once again a fairly obvious one: the basic power unit planned initially, with its output of 110 kW (150 bhp), would not have set the TT apart sufficiently from the more powerful models in the A3 range and identified it as a thoroughbred sports car.

In view of this, the decision to give even the basic TT model a 132 kW (180 bhp) four-cylinder engine was a logical one. For the top model, a 165 kW (225 bhp) engine had to be developed in order to give the TT the performance that would propel it to the forefront of the sports coupé market segment.

The development of a totally new car calls for so many complex questions to be answered that the project leader has to have a limited but adequate number of specialists at his disposal, on whom he can rely for a series of solutions to detail matters. Stefan Härdl puts it this way: "We knew from the start that we could only prepare the TT design study for production if three conditions were satisfied. First of all, the production car had to comply as closely as possible with the original study. We didn't want people reproaching us for having turned a fascinating idea into mediocre reality merely to suit the constraints of series budget limits, and thirdly the whole process had to take place away from the regular technical development facilities in Ingolstadt, which were already working hard on the forthcoming model programme and had no scope for handling an additional project such as this."

At this point the miracle of the Audi TT began to take shape. Not a single line from the two original prototypes reached the start of series production unchanged. The development process optimised every detail, and yet the TT's unique character was successfully retained.

Technical

The basic engine, rated at 132 kW (180 bhp), can be identified visually by its single charge-air intercooler.

"We drafted the whole car out afresh", the members of the team confirm today, "but it lost none of its fine qualities. On the contrary, we improved on them still further!"

This minor miracle was largely due to the rare degree of harmony that prevailed between the designers and the technical teams. Stefan Härdl: "We all pledged ourselves to work an extra night shift rather than leave a problem unsolved or accept a compromise that would have reduced the impact of this outstanding design."

The stylists had a major part to play in maintaining this personal harmony. Their basic work at the prototype development stage, however, had been so successful that scarcely any revisions were needed, and these only for unavoidable technical reasons.

Such an impressive spirit of cooperation, with both groups dedicated to upholding the absolute character of the design through every subsequent stage of readying it for production, is one of the main reasons for the Audi TT having retained the originality that created such a sensation when it was first seen.

All too often, design studies mutate into road-going models at the expense of much of their elegance and originality, whereas in this case everyone concerned was dedicated to minimising the visual changes that had to be applied to the TT to equip it for series production.

The need to perform much of the development work away from the company's main technical centre – though of course without transferring any key responsibilities to outside providers – enabled the key group responsible for the new car to be kept small. Whereas a new high-volume model can call for the formation of up to 160 specialised teams, the TT was prepared for production by only five simultaneous-engineering (SE) groups, who were authorised to borrow the services of other specialists when tackling details of the design.

With this small but highly effective key team, the TT project was tackled at a high level of concentration, with scarcely any hierarchical levels among the members. Every specialised area had its own highly qualified representative who could speak directly to the colleagues responsible for parallel areas when necessary. In this way, urgent problems were never postponed or less than ideal solutions settled for.

As if to make the whole TT project even more stimulating for its participants, the time schedule was unbelievably tight. Audi's chief executive Franz-Josef Paefgen wanted to drive the first pre-production TT himself in the 40th week of 1996 – the end of September. In other words the team had precisely a year at its disposal if the first car was to roll out on schedule.

For Paefgen to be able to take the wheel of the first TT Roadster only three weeks later was a further sporting challenge which the members of the team decided to accept as well.

A timetable like this really deserves to be stamped "mission impossible", but in this case the impossible was achieved without even taking a little longer: "The group that worked on the TT was small and totally identified with the task of developing the Coupé quickly and producing it at a reasonable price, without sacrificing any of its innate charm. This was our dream, and in order to fulfil it we thought about the TT and nothing else for the entire three years."

From the technical standpoint, the first task after the "IAA" exhibition was to compare the two prototypes section by section with volume-production needs. The interior of the car was subjected to the same treatment from mid-1996 onwards.

To ensure high torsional rigidity, the roof frame and sills of the TT Coupé's body are even stronger than on saloon-car models.

Both prototypes, as we have seen, had been built on the Audi A3 and Golf IV platform after shortening it by 90 millimetres. This length reduction was retained for the production car, though in the course of development work the body itself grew in length by 30 millimetres. Just three of these were added to the front overhang in order to accommodate a US-style bumper. The remaining 27 millimetres were due to slight restyling of the TT's rear end, which was regarded as insufficiently well-defined in the original sketches.

The technical experts accepted this change without objection, and indeed from that time on only one change was made to the production car's appearance for technical reasons. This related to the air inlet for the charge-air intercooler, which had to be enlarged slightly to satisfy the new top engine's voracious demand for cooling air. It may well be that no outsider was consciously aware of this minor styling change, though the car magazine *auto motor und sport* did in fact write in a May 1998 issue: "Seen directly from the front, the production TT Coupé even looks a tad more powerful than the design study, and has a hint of extra elegance at the rear. In particular when shod with 225/45 tyres on 17-inch wheels, this 2+2-seater, which is only 4.04 metres long but 1.76 metres wide and a mere 1.35 metres high, crouches most impressively on the road."

Important steps on computer aided design

To give the body structure the high level of torsional rigidity that is particularly important in a sports car, the sills and roof frame were of new design. Since the time schedule only allowed 28 months for the work, the main requirements in the static and dynamic stress analysis, refinement and safety areas were analysed and confirmed by computer simulation well before even the first actual prototype had been completed. Stefan Härdl: "Without modern high-performance computers we would never have achieved results that were confirmed to the last detail by our practical tests later." It still gives him pleasure to recall that during the crash-rig tests "the body crumpled at precisely the points which the computer had identified during our design work."

The main problem when these computer calculations were being performed was to uphold Audi's strict, no-compromise construction standards without being compelled to alter any visual aspects of the design.

A major challenge was represented by the half-height B-posts and also by the very large rear hatch. Generous roof frame cross-sections and sills 40 millimetres deeper than on the A models enabled body rigidity to be increased to an outstanding level worthy of a true sports car. With only a minimum weight penalty, torsional rigidity was boosted to the high figure of 19,000 Nm per degree and excellent protection assured in side impact collisions and rollover accidents.

While one section of the team dealt with the chassis, others were working in parallel on the suspension.

"The first show cars had an unmodified A3 front axle and a modified quattro axle layout at the rear. We rescued the components from a road-test car that was due to be scrapped", Ralf-Gerhard Willner recalls. "But obviously this was only an interim solution to get the cars mobile. For the production version we initially planned to use A3 running gear with modified spring and shock absorber settings specific to the TT. By the time the first pre-production car had to be presented to the board of management in that notorious Week 40, however, we had established that the Coupé didn't handle significantly better than a regular Audi A3 with this choice of suspension."

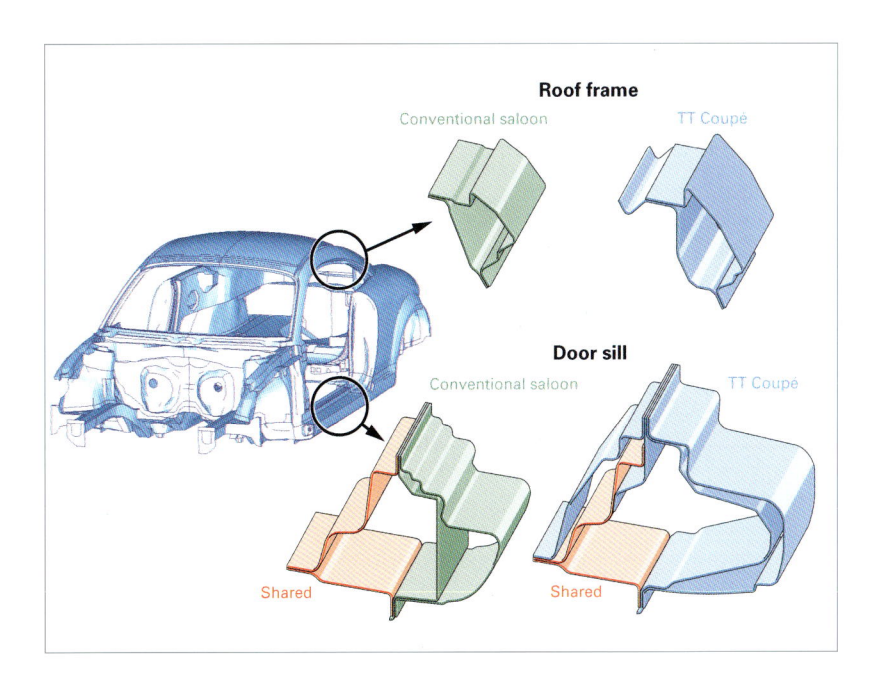

Technical

The state of the art

The objective *of chassis and suspension development was to evolve from the latest transverse-engined passenger car principles a design worthy of a modern sports car.*

It was also found that the brake system would have to be considerably revised in order to match the new model's genuine sports-car performance.

A new work area had suddenly opened up, and the task of producing completely revised running gear unique to the TT had to be tackled. The short wheelbase was an excellent starting point, together with the wide track, large wheels with wide tyres, the low centre of gravity and the firm suspension settings. They were all ideal preconditions for "evolving a suspension layout suitable for a modern sports car from the latest principles used for transverse-engined passenger cars", as Technical Director Dr. Werner Mischke describes this task.

For the front suspension, *McPherson spring struts with a new forged wishbone were adopted (upper picture). At the rear, Audi decided to install a combined trailing arm and double-wishbone layout with separate spring and shock absorber mountings; the gas-filled shock absorbers were positioned at an angle (lower picture).*

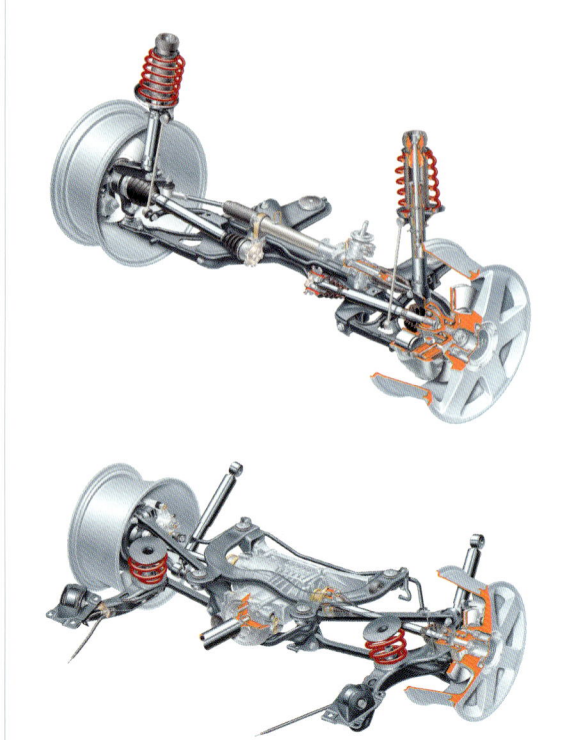

For the front wheels, McPherson struts were chosen and new, forged wishbones developed. To make full use of the space provided in association with the 17-inch wheels, the suspension kinematics were thoroughly revised with the emphasis on high agility and precision, as would befit a sports car of this calibre. The wide 1,527-millimetre track and the anti-roll bar with its 1:1 outer-end mounting at the suspension strut helped to keep body roll well under control, since every millimetre of spring travel was transferred in the same ratio into rotary movement of the anti-roll bar. The camber and toe angles were altered to match the TT's character. When the suspension is compressed, it adopts only a slight toe-out position, so that the car's handling remains largely neutral.

The engineers' final choice of rear suspension was a combined trailing arm and double wishbone layout, with the springs and shock absorbers mounted separately and the gas-filled shock absorbers inclined at a considerable angle. The axle beam itself is attached to the body by means of two large rubber-to-metal elements which also perform a guiding function and are tilted at 25 degrees to the TT's transverse axis. This layout, together with the directional compliance effect built into the axle mountings, helps to eliminate undesirable self-steering effects when the wheels are exposed to lateral forces, and to suppress the transmission of road noise to the body.

52 | 53

Between the 180 horsepower front-wheel-drive version of the Audi TT and its sister-models with four-wheel drive there are, however, other minor differences: for instance, the former has a tubular anti-roll bar welded to the rear axle, whereas the TT quattro's anti-roll bar is connected to the wheel hubs by separate rods.

The TT's power-assisted steering has a very direct ratio, with a characteristic that once again matches the demands of the sports car driver very well, ensuring optimum road feel and high steering precision at all speeds.

Such excellent ingredients in the running-gear mix naturally formed an ideal basis for installation of the more powerful engines that were considered to be necessary. The first prototype used the A3's turbocharged engine as its power source, but as we have seen, the need for more power was soon obvious. It was therefore decided to fit the 132 kW (180 bhp) inline four-cylinder engine to the basic TT, and develop a 165 kW (225 bhp) unit for the top model.

This power boost meant extra work for the technical development centre, which was asked to prepare a new 165 kW version of the engine. This task clearly had to be handled by the Ingolstadt plant's central technical development facility, despite the fact that it already had quite enough on its plate.

Stefan Härdl comments: "The design concept called for a transverse-mounted engine. This enabled the front overhang to be kept very short, but there was still space for charge-air intercoolers and the air conditioning condenser at the left and right of the main radiator. Naturally, the demand for a very compact engine was in itself a challenge, since high specific output means that various peripheral components have to be increased in size to cope with the additional power; this was certainly true of the charge-air intercoolers, which were quite difficult to integrate into the overall package without interfering with access to other components."
In this way two engines took shape on the basis of the existing 110 kW (150 bhp) four-cylinder unit, and proved capable of imparting the desired degree of temperament to the new Audi TT. The 132 kW (180 bhp) version of the four-cylinder engine, as used in the basic TT models, incorporates a KKK Type K03 turbocharger. Together with the relatively high compression ratio of 9.5:1, this means high efficiency combined with moderate fuel consumption.

Technical

An ingenious device

The maximum torque of this engine version is 235 Nm, available over a broad engine-speed range from 1,950 to 5,000 rpm. Both the front- and four-wheel drive versions of this TT accelerate from 0 to 100 km/h in 7.4 seconds, the former reaching a top speed of 228 km/h, the quattro only just behind it at 226 km/h.

As we have already seen briefly, the 165 kW (225 bhp) engine needed more extensive design revision before this exceptionally high output could be obtained from a swept volume of only 1,781 cc. The first step was to uprate the main bearings in the engine block; the pistons were also strengthened and the compression ratio reduced from 9.5 to 8.9:1. The five-valve cylinder head was retained, but with very shallow-angle inlet ports so that a tumble effect was created in the combustion chamber, parallel to the crankshaft axis.

This tumble effect creates a controlled amount of turbulence in the mixture flow and thus has a highly favourable influence on the combustion rate and therefore also on power output and smoothness.

Since the air temperature in the intake manifold also has a significant effect on combustion efficiency, effective charge-air cooling using two intercoolers was considered to be vital. Despite the high level of boost adopted for this engine, more than 80 percent intercooler efficiency is achieved at top speed.

The engineers solved two problems in one very neatly in this area: the connecting pipe between the two charge-air intercoolers is also used as a stiffening tube between the front body side members; this reduces vibration and lowers the noise level.

The airflow cross-sections were increased in order to handle the larger volumes of cooling and combustion air which the more powerful engine needs. In addition, the KKK Type K04 turbocharger and exhaust manifold form part of an entirely redesigned exhaust system, again with a view to ensuring optimum cylinder filling and scavenging.

Before the air reaches the combustion chambers it is compressed to about 2 bar above atmospheric pressure in the turbocharger. This increase in pressure, and the added influence of high outside temperatures, heat up the air. In the two intercoolers, which are arranged in series, it is cooled

Technical

again, so that when it reaches the intake manifold it is no more than 20 degrees higher than the ambient temperature. This practical principle is one of the main reasons why this 1.8-litre engine is able to develop its impressive 225 horsepower.

The engine, which reaches its maximum power output at 5,900 rpm, complies in full with the EU 3 D exhaust emission limits. Considerable effort had to be expended to ensure this desirable state of affairs: the 165 kW version, for instance, has an engine-driven secondary air pump which helps to keep it below the statutory emission levels. Fresh air is taken directly from the air cleaner and pumped into the exhaust ports, where an after-burning effect takes place. The resulting thermal energy is used to heat up the catalytic converter so that it begins to operate efficiently and purify the exhaust gas very soon after the engine has started.

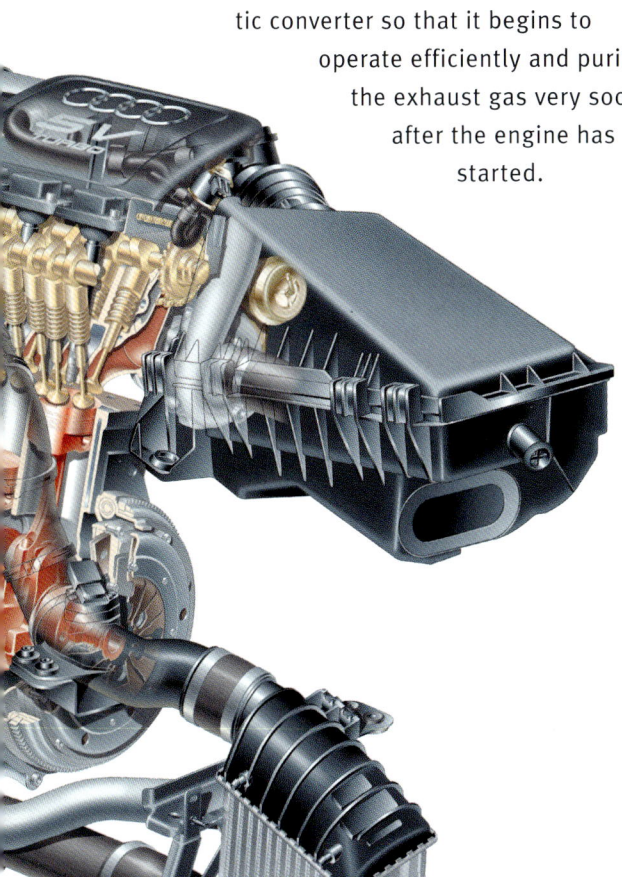

A sports car, of course, is driven with all the senses active, and Audi's development team therefore undertook a multi-stage process – "sound tuning" – with a view to making their sports car sound as splendid as it looks and as it performs. The resulting sound is unmistakably dynamic, yet neither penetrating nor aggressive; in accordance with the law, it isn't excessively loud either.

The acoustic development work led to another visible distinguishing feature between the two TT versions: the top model with its 165 kW engine has two boldly styled exhaust tailpipes, whereas the two 132 kW versions are content with one.

To return for the moment to the more powerful engine: its high torque of 280 Nm over a wide engine-speed range from 2,200 to 5,500 rpm is largely due to the use of the very latest electronic engine management system, known as Motronic MW 7.5. This adaptive system performs a most impressive range of functions: throttle butterfly opening angle, boost pressure regulation, sequential fuel injection with air mass measurement by hot film sensor, mapped-characteristic, solid-state HT ignition using individual coils, cylinder-selective knock control with two sensors and a "lambda probe" to act as an oxygen sensor. It has still further regulating functions to perform in conjunction with EDS, ASR and the controlled torque distribution unit incorporated into the quattro driveline.

A power output of 165 kW (225 bhp), no less, is obtained from the top version of the 1.8-litre four-cylinder engine, equivalent to a most impressive specific output per litre. Two charge-air intercoolers contribute to this exceptional power flow, by keeping the temperature of the air entering the intake manifold down to no more than 20 degrees above ambient temperature.

The project team (continued):
Left hand group (from left to right): Holger Baumann, Helmut Adam, Sigbert Scholtyssek; sitting in the car: Stefan Härdl (left) and Claus Haverkamp; seated in front (from left to right): Romuald Stukan, Jörg-Urs Fuchs, Klaus-Dietrich Krieger; on the right: Thomas Rossie.

Speaking at the TT presentation, Audi's technical director Dr. Werner Mischke explained the highly complex functions of this Motronic engine management system as follows: "In simplified terms we could say that the engine management interprets the driver's power requirement as expressed by movement of the accelerator pedal, then decides how to satisfy it as quickly as possible, using a minimum amount of fuel."

The system adjusts the throttle opening angle, boost pressure and ignition timing to obtain this optimum result. The throttle, incidentally, is of the "drive by wire" type, with no mechanical link, not even a wire cable, between the accelerator pedal and the engine, but an electronic circuit which performs the same task. The throttle butterfly responds immediately and opens to the angle which corresponds to the engine's load situation.

The engine management system is adaptive, that is to say capable of learning how to respond in given circumstances; in the same way it adapts to variations in fuel quality, by choosing the best combination of boost pressure, torque and ignition timing.

A truly remarkable engine, and one which incidentally tips the scales at only 130.5 kilograms. The next task was to team it up with an adequate gearbox; in the event, a new unit known as the MQ 350.6 was specially developed for transverse installation in both front- and four-wheel drive cars. The targets were to provide six forward gears and handle an engine torque of up to 350 Nm.

To make this possible, a housing of greatly reduced overall length and a three-shaft layout were chosen. Without the clutch casing, the gearbox is 268 millimetres long; at its narrowest point, adjacent to the body side member, it is only 249 millimetres wide.

The compact three-shaft layout has numerous advantages: greater flexibility in the choice of ratios, high efficiency, lightweight construction despite the high strength and operating-life demands – and last but not least, shorter shift movements and a smooth lever action.

"Our team constantly asked itself what features an authentic sports car should possess, and one of the most frequent wishes was for a small gear lever with short, precisely defined shift movements", Ralf-Gerhard Willner remembers. "We therefore asked our colleagues in the transmission development area to keep this wish in mind, and they have achieved precisely the result we were hoping for!"

Technical

The concept has influenced every single component

"They are another fine example of the enthusiasm that this car generated right through the company: the desire to build the kind of car one would like to have in one's own garage at home."

To satisfy the demand for a precise, light-action shift, the first, second and third gears have Smith triple-cone synchromesh, the upper three gears Borg-Warner high-performance single-cone synchromesh.

Reverse gear is equipped with an optimised form of external-cone synchromesh, and lever movements are transmitted to the gearbox by a wire cable mechanism. This has the advantage of keeping the gearbox and the gear lever assembly mechanically decoupled, so that very little vibration can be transmitted between them. Altogether, this high-performance gearbox (without the attached bevel gear housing) weighs only 48.5 kilograms including its oil content in the form used for front-wheel drive cars; the four-wheel-drive version tips the scales at 47 kilograms.

To achieve such low weights, the housing is made of magnesium and the shafts are hollow-drilled. Once again, the computer must share the praise for this convincing design, since it enabled the finite-element method to be used to optimise the weight and strength of the new gearbox.

In the early days, it was planned to build the TT only with the quattro driveline, but before long the logic of offering the car with front-wheel drive when powered by the 132 kW (180 bhp) engine became accepted. This less powerful car features the successful Audi five-speed gearbox.

A concept calling for a highly agile, lively sports car clearly has its effects on just about every individual component: this is evident when we examine the permanent four-wheel-drive layout used on the two quattro versions of the TT.

As we have seen, the transverse engine contributes greatly to the compact overall size of the TT, with its extremely short body overhangs. However, the transverse engine also needed specially matched power distribution to distribute torque between the front and rear axles. The TT quattro is the first model in the Audi programme to use an electro-hydraulically controlled torque distribution system.

Developed jointly with the Swedish manufacturer Haldex, this is a particularly compact device with incredibly rapid response times, and therefore ideal for use in a sports car such as the TT. It alters the torque distribution even before the difference in front and rear propeller shaft rotation has reached 45 degrees.

If slip occurs at the front wheels, for example, so that optimum traction can no longer be guaranteed, the torque distribution system acts immediately and diverts a precisely controlled additional proportion of engine torque to the rear axle.

The control process is so rapid that the road wheels have not covered more than 25 centimetres before it takes effect.

Four-wheel drive in reverse gear too

The electronically controlled hydraulic multi-plate clutch is installed between the propeller shaft and the rear-axle differential. Inside the housing is a set of clutch plates running in an oilbath. The plates can be pressed together by varying the hydraulic pressure, and are thus able to transmit a varying amount of torque to the rear wheels. An electric preload pump ensures that the clutch can respond instantly: the higher the pressure, the greater the proportion of torque redistributed to the rear wheels.

There is no fixed rate at which the torque transfer process from front to rear takes place. This is a dynamic system, with torque levels controlled by a number of different parameters.

Pressure at the clutch operating piston is maintained by two axial-piston pumps. These are driven by a swashplate, which begins to take effect as soon as there is a difference between the input and output shafts. The pressure can be varied steplessly by an electronically controlled valve. The associated control unit analyses a variety of information, including wheel rotating speeds, engine speed and engine torque.

The system has a memorised software program that enables it to respond to the driver's intentions: for instance, the clutch disengages if an ABS-controlled brake application is detected, so that no front-rear torque transfer takes place and the ABS regulating system can operate correctly.

The electrically operated multi-plate clutch is located between the propeller shaft and the rear-axle differential. An electric preload pump maintains pressure so that the clutch can respond quickly. The higher the pressure, the more torque the clutch can redistribute to the rear axle.

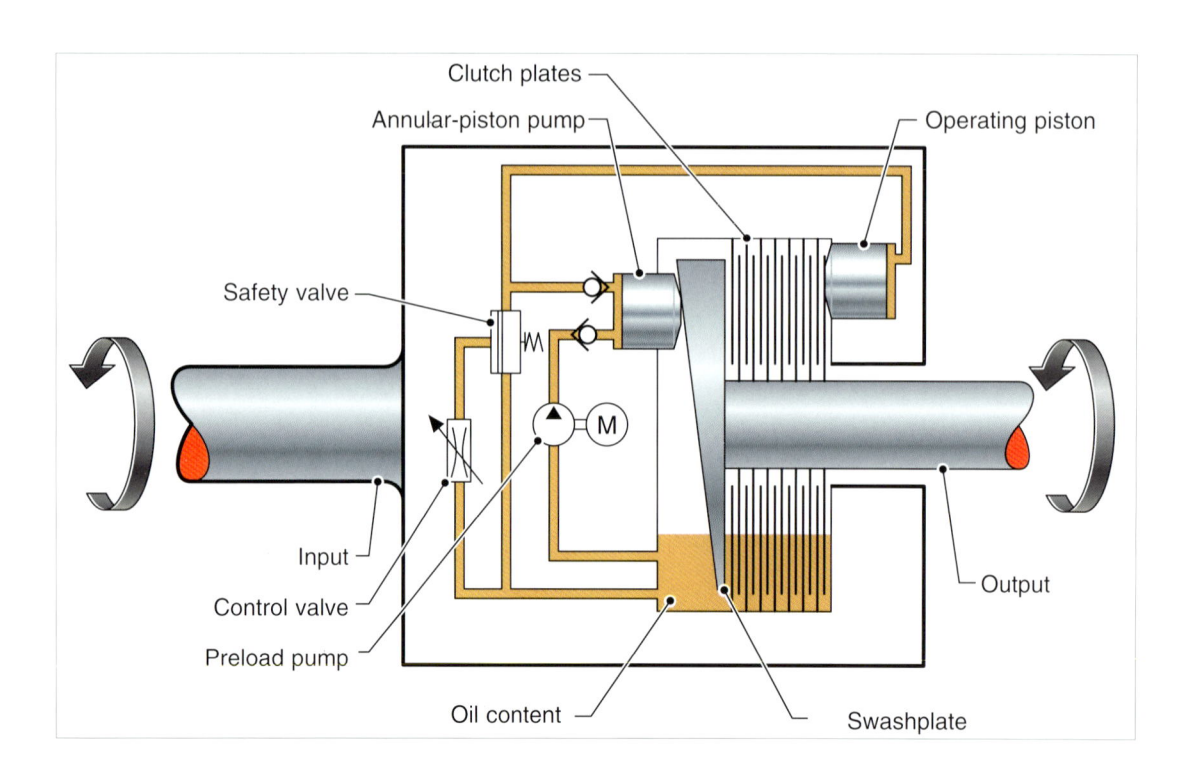

- Clutch plates
- Annular-piston pump
- Operating piston
- Safety valve
- Input
- Control valve
- Preload pump
- Oil content
- Output
- Swashplate

Technical

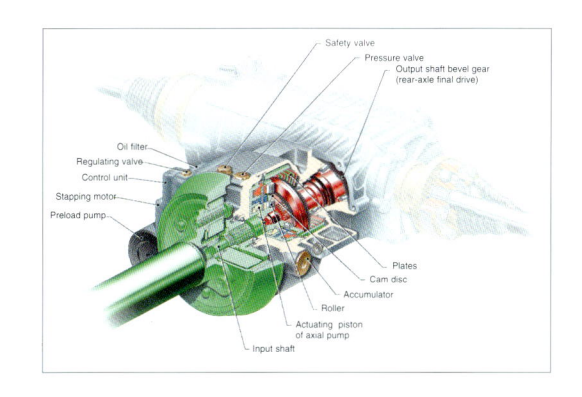

It's interesting to note that this system remains active when the car is driven in reverse, so that maximum traction is always available. The four-wheel-drive version of the TT is notable for its mild, consistent road behaviour when the engine is on the overrun. This is important, for example, if the driver releases the accelerator pedal abruptly while cornering fast. Locating the multi-plate clutch at the rear in a front-engined car also improves the weight distribution, and makes a further contribution to the TT's outstanding dynamic stability.

To ensure the best possible traction in all situations, TT models are not only fitted with the best four-wheel-drive system currently available but also with other "electronic co-pilots" that enhance dynamic stability and safety: a modern anti-lock braking system (ABS), an electronic differential lock (EDL) for the front axle and electronic braking-pressure distribution (EBD). In addition, the front-wheel-drive version with 132 kW (180 bhp) engine has traction control (ASR).

A high-performance car clearly needs correspondingly good brakes, and the TT therefore has discs at all wheels. At the front they are 312 millimetres, at the rear 256 millimetres in diameter. The front discs are of the ventilated type with both engine options; the top model has these at the rear as well.

The fist-type rear brake calipers are made of aluminium, to save weight and reduce unsprung mass at the wheel, so that vibration is reduced and dynamic progress assured.

It was a remarkable achievement to complete development work on the Coupé, including all its complex technical features, within only two years and four months. For Peter Schreyer, who as Audi's design chief was naturally informed about the activities of the small, dedicated TT team, there was something almost obsessive about the search for the "absolute" in every pencil line, every technical feature and every equipment detail:

"We wanted to build the 'pure sports car' and reduce the task to achieving a new blend of technical achievement and driving pleasure. Our engineers and designers all pulled together with the aim of fulfilling our dream with as few changes as possible and at an acceptable price."

As we have already seen, the development team was quite small, and made up of groups working in a highly independent way, though with access at any time to the resources of the main technical development and product planning departments if specialised knowledge was needed.

The multi-plate clutch that distributes engine torque between the front and rear axles has no fixed operating characteristic – it is part of a dynamic system which regulates the torque split according to a large number of different parameters.

Plenty of room to manoeuvre

The TT Coupé and TT Roadster already comply with forthcoming European crash legislation, thanks to the lengthy and complex computer simulation work that was carried out successfully by the development team.

Those whose task it has been to chronicle the progress of the Audi TT know that about six people, no more, were responsible for its development. The successive development stages benefited from the high degree of independence granted to them. They monitored their own activity and in due course presented the various stages on the car's road to production maturity to those responsible for taking major corporate decisions.

Stefan Härdl: "It wasn't exactly an easy task, in view of Audi's high standards of quality. But the freedom of action we enjoyed was something other developers can only dream of!"

It would be all too easy to record details of the development team's work as if it were a simple linear progression from one day to the next. In actual fact many activities were taking place in parallel at any given time, all hopefully under careful control. Chassis, suspension, engine, gearbox, electronics, the car's interior, production planning – details began to slot into place in all corners of the jigsaw puzzle. Slowly but surely the first chassis and bodies were built up and the first power train components manufactured, while elsewhere work proceeded, for instance, on the ABS system or on new seats for the TT.

Many external tasks also called for advice from the various specialists, but some tasks, notably the car's crash-test behaviour, had to be tackled within the company.

As we have already seen, the TT body gains much of its remarkable rigidity from the generous cross-sections of its roof frame and door sills, and it is this property that forms such an excellent basis for the running gear.

Admittedly, a rigid bodyshell isn't the only desirable factor, since modern cars have to satisfy increasingly stringent crash test requirements, which means that programmed crumple zones have to be incorporated.

Lengthy computer simulations were needed to arrive at a structure that complies with every relevant safety regulation. "Admittedly, we're never content merely to satisfy current legislation", says Dr. Werner Mischke. "We insisted that the TT should pass the far tougher internal crash tests that Audi includes in its development programmes."

In some cases these have been suggested by consumer organisations or leading car magazines, or represent legislation that is not due to come into force for some years. "But in all these crash tests, the TT's safety systems demonstrated their protective effect extremely well."

Technical

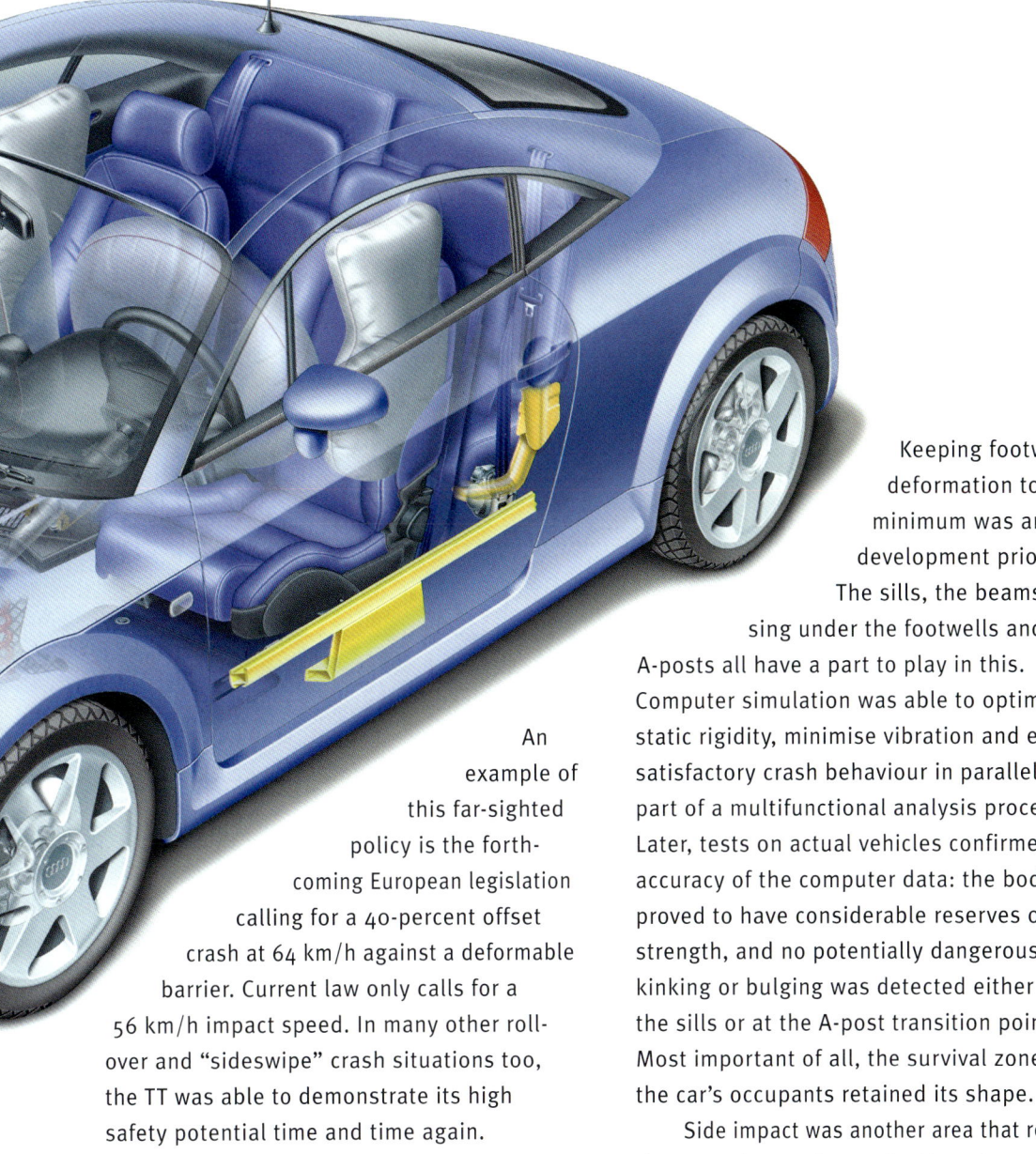

An example of this far-sighted policy is the forthcoming European legislation calling for a 40-percent offset crash at 64 km/h against a deformable barrier. Current law only calls for a 56 km/h impact speed. In many other rollover and "sideswipe" crash situations too, the TT was able to demonstrate its high safety potential time and time again.

Similar work was devoted to crash protection in the Roadster, which has two roll hoops that not only add visual interest but are in fact an integral structural element, contributing to the safety and rigidity of the car's open-top body. A substantial windscreen frame with double anchorages inside the A-posts and a high-strength steel tube system are also used to enhance occupant protection on the Roadster.

Keeping footwell deformation to a minimum was another development priority. The sills, the beams passing under the footwells and the A-posts all have a part to play in this. Computer simulation was able to optimise static rigidity, minimise vibration and ensure satisfactory crash behaviour in parallel, as part of a multifunctional analysis process. Later, tests on actual vehicles confirmed the accuracy of the computer data: the body proved to have considerable reserves of strength, and no potentially dangerous kinking or bulging was detected either at the sills or at the A-post transition points. Most important of all, the survival zone for the car's occupants retained its shape.

Side impact was another area that received the most thorough examination. Once again, computer simulation enabled all the parameters of relevance in a crash, such as the door structure and even the interior trim materials, to be modified at a very early stage.

To reduce side intrusion speed as much as possible, a stuctural element linking the half-height B-post to the rear seat crossmember was introduced. The combination of sturdy impact-absorbing beams in the doors, made from high-strength aluminium, and the torsionally resistant door sills, enabled the side structure to be given a carefully controlled level of resistance to external forces. The doors themselves are designed to share the energy absorption process with other body elements. In addition, side airbags protect the thorax and head areas of the occupants' bodies.

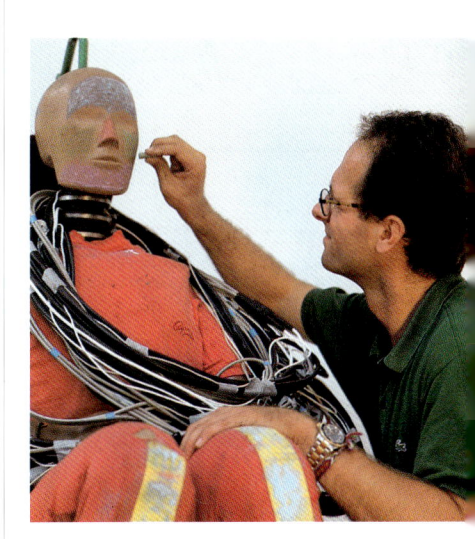

"The outsider can scarcely be expected to grasp just how much time and money we save by using the computer for our calculations", says Stefan Härdl. In his view there is no doubt that "in earlier times many vastly expensive hand-built prototypes would have been destroyed in equally costly crash tests in so far as these had already been developed, without achieving anything like the standard of occupant safety that the TT can offer." In other words, although safety standards have risen enormously, it has proved possible to absorb at least part of the additional cost by adopting modern methods.

One of these essential requirements during body development for this particular car was for the quality of the design to remain intact. This proved to be far from easy, since the TT derives so much of its fascination from the smooth, consistent nature of its styling. The plastic bumpers, for instance, were successfully mounted flush with the body with no visible projections, and even the flaps for the headlight cleaning jets and the mirrors are not just attached on top of the body panels, but integrated perfectly into them so that the usual seals needed to eliminate minor tolerances can be dispensed with. The mirrors, for instance, really do seem to grow out of the door panels.

Aesthetic considerations are of course all very well, but customer benefit always has to be given ultimate priority.

Large-area underfloor panels at the front and rear, and a spoiler ahead of the wheels, have cut aerodynamic drag by about ten percent as well as lowering lift forces at the front and rear axles.

The bumper system achieves one of the best values for any car in this class – type rating 19 according to German insurers, and despite use of these neat, flush-fitting assemblies the headlights, the radiator and the air conditioning condenser remained undamaged in the standard crash test.

It proved more complicated to solve the technical production problems that arose at the sharp-edged transition from the base of the roof to the side panel close to the C-post. This is precisely the point at which the roof and the rear side panels part company in a dramatic way, and therefore the joint line had to be perfect, but no conventional production method seemed appropriate. The last thing the stylists wanted to do was to attach a chrome or plastic strip in order to cover up the seam, since this would simply not have been sufficiently "absolute".

The problem was handed over by the SE team originally responsible to a new group from Bamberg University, which was asked to develop a new production technique that would permit Audi's bodyshell quality standards to be reliably achieved. Ten people worked on this new technique for a period of two years, with no real guarantee that they would succeed in delivering the magic formula before the deadline. Laser-beam brazing proved to be the answer that yielded the desired bold, clean joint line at this vitally important area of the body.

Look – no rear spoiler!

Optimum surface quality, low and carefully controlled heat input to avoid thermal distortion in the microstructure, a high-strength joint and reliable processing: all these requirements are satisfied by the new brazing method, which is also ecologically acceptable and takes place without any flux, under an inert gas, to prevent corrosion from occuring.

To quote Stefan Härdl again: "This too is evidence of the unusual technical steps we were prepared to take in order to preserve the integrity of the design."

Another design-led decision was the use of sheet steel for the side skirts, which are a separate and distinct styling element on this car, instead of the usual add-on plastic components. It was felt that plastic skirts would have been too long and would therefore have had to include an unsightly expansion joint.

Other problems were solved too: The TT's founding fathers were convinced right from the outset that such ravishing outlines ought not to be desecrated by attaching spoilers to the body. An alternative approach had to be adopted in order to keep aerodynamic lift down to a minimum on a sports car that is, after all, capable of reaching speeds of up to 240 km/h.

After several hundred hours of wind-tunnel testing and computer analysis, the aerodynamics team succeeded in developing a most ingenious shape for the underside of the body, with large-area cover panels at the front and rear and a spoiler in front of the wheels to reduce wind resistance. These measures improved the drag coefficient by about ten percent and at the same time reduced lift at both the front and rear axles.

The entire under-surface of the body was developed with the aid of a totally new wind-tunnel simulation technique originally used for racing cars. Despite its generously sized wheels, which themselves account for about 25 percent of total wind resistance, and the large openings needed to feed air to a hungry, powerful engine, the TT achieves an excellent c_D value for a sports car of 0.34 and has a frontal area of A=1.99 square metres.

Detail refinement in the wind tunnel had other benefits too: despite the absence of rain channels at the sides of the windscreen, scarcely any water is deposited on the side windows.

After systematic aerodynamic tests, the A-posts of the body were raised very slightly.

Technical

Putting on the style

At the rear, the spoiler lip was reshaped to keep dirt clear of the rear window, so that the wiper can be dispensed with.

And of course, one of the unceasing aims was to keep wind noise down to a low level.

The Coupé's frameless side windows are a particular challenge in terms of avoiding wind noise, which therefore has to be tackled and minimised at source, for example at the outside mirrors. The aero-acoustic standard is comparable with large luxury cars such as the A6 or A8.

The perfection with which the design study's outlines were translated into production sheet metal naturally had to be paralleled by equally thorough attention to the car's interior. Times have certainly changed: sports cars used to be noted for their spartan equipment and trim, but today's customer is looking for many if not all of the features of a luxury saloon car or grand tourer. The TT is ready and waiting to fulfil such wishes, all the way from radio-operated remote control and central locking to illuminated make-up mirrors. If the customer wants it, then it can be supplied! One thing was very important to the designers, though: the materials that the TT's occupants see also had to be pleasant to touch.

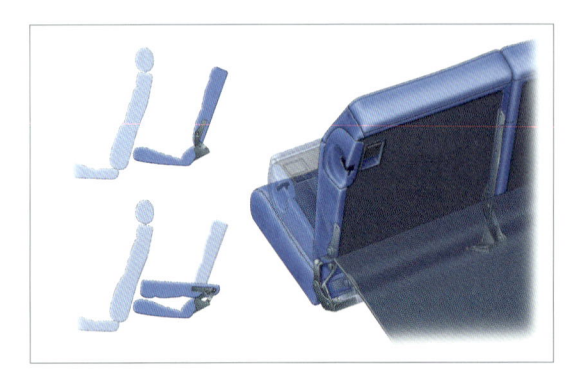

At the TT presentation, Peter Schreyer was heard to sum this up very succinctly: "If it looks like aluminium, it has to be aluminium:" He went on: "The TT is the first car in which aluminium is not only an innovative structural material but also a pleasant, distinguished functional and design element. This is equally true of the aluminium rings round the air outlets, the steering wheel, the gear lever and the switches for the heated seats."

The loving care that the designers and technicians devoted to these details can be seen for instance in the rotary controls that replace the customary pushbuttons for the air conditioning. They are used to adjust the temperature and blower speed, and give the user a clearly defined feedback as to the switch position that has been selected.

Technical

The TT has a specially developed fully-automatic climate control system that keeps the individually selected temperature inside the car constant in any situation. A sensor using SMD electronics is integrated into the automatic air conditionong system, and measures the temperature inside the car at the airflow from a micro-blower.

Other factors influencing the final value are the outside temperature, that of the air emerging from the outlets and the intensity of the sun, which measured by a mono-sensor on the dash panel. The signal from this sun sensor is used to correct the overall temperature level inside the car and to boost blower output if necessary by altering the supply voltage to its motor.

From the four measured values the system derives the signals tranmitted to the four blower adjusting motors. Air distribution and blower output can also be varied manually by departing from the fully-automatic operating mode, and in addition the car's occupants can switch from fresh air input to recirculated air, or choose an economy function.

The switch for the heated seats, which are a standard feature, extends slightly from the dash panel when finger pressure is applied, so that the temperature can be preselected. Up to six light-emitting diodes in the domed switch surround indicate the heat level – separately for driver and front passenger, a technically ingenious and visually attractive operating principle.

Another highlight of the interior equipment and trim are the sports seats, which have combined leather and alcantara upholstery as a standard feature. To ensure the correct seated position that is particularly important in a sports car, both the front seats are contoured to accommodate the occupant's body, and continuously adjustable.

As an optional extra, the TT Roadster can be obtained with the "Authentic" package, in which the occupants take their seats in an all-leather environment that resembles nothing more than an oversize baseball glove. In addition to the conventional sewn seams, the sides of the seats are woven together with a leather thong, for all the world like the mocassins the Red Indians wear.

For the first time on the TT, aluminium is used not only as a technically innovative construction material but also as an agreeable, dignified functional and design element. An ingenious four-pivot mechanism causes the rear seat backs to disappear partly under the flat load-area floor; the full range of front seat adjustment remains available.

Load up and away

A concentrated high-tech package operates under the bonnet of the TT Roadster. Inside the car and in the luggage compartment, there is ample space for the two occupants and their luggage.

There is yet another way in which the TT Coupé differs favorably from all its rivals: for a sports car, it has a satisfyingly large luggage compartment holding 220 litres on quattro cars and as much as 272 litres if the TT has front-wheel drive. Thanks to a tailgate that extends well up into the roof, it's easy to make good use of this luggage-carrying capacity.

And if the rear seat backs are folded, the available space goes up to approximately 490 litres – with an entirely flat load surface, since the seat backs partly disappear under the floor thank to a cleverly designed four-pivot mechanism. The space gained in this way also enables the full range of front-seat adjustment to be retained.

The TT is of course available with a range of optional extras, including for instance larger wheels and tyres for the 132 kW version. But this is not all: a driver information system can be specified, xenon headlights and even all-leather upholstery and trim (at no extra charge incidentally).

Technical

For superb on-board audio there are four systems specially matched to the TT's interior, notably the BOSE Sound System, which has a total of seven loudspeakers including a centerfill unit in the dash panel, a four-channel amplifier rated at 175 Watts and four equalisers.

Before the TT could be unveiled at its world premiere, no fewer than thirty stage-one prototypes were built – both Coupés and Roadsters, starting immediately after that ominous deadline in Week 40.

In March 1997 work began on assembling the next 35 hand-built prototypes for construction phase 2. Each of these had its own contribution to make in the process of tracking down and eliminating possible weak points in the design step by step.

It was obvious from the start that the TT Roadster's soft top would have to be given a simple, easily operated linkage so that it could be opened and closed with one hand. A power-operated soft top is also available.

Working towards a classic product

The first major hurdle was taken in 1996, when crash tests began with a bare bodyshell and every crumple zone proved in reality to conform perfectly with the forecasts obtained by computer simulation. For Stefan Härdl, this is confirmation of how much can be achieved with the fascinating new methods of computer-aided design: "We only had just over two years for development to series-production maturity – even four or five years earlier, we would never have been able to achieve such perfection in so short a time."

The Roadster was in fact developed in parallel with the Coupé, though thanks to the high proportion of identical parts this task proved to be much less difficult than the outside observer might suspect.

The roadster naturally had to be given an additional subframe braced to the body, as a means of compensating for the lack of a fixed roof panel. Extra bulkhead plates were installed too, with the result that the Roadster's torsional rigidity is quite remarkably high.

"We could see that only a classic roadster with a simple folding soft top would do!" says Stefan Härdl. For him and his colleagues it was important for the driver or front passenger to be able to open or close the soft top in a single movement. It was therefore given a single centrally located handle which also locks and unlocks the catches at the front. Those who prefer a hint of extra luxury can of course order an electrically operated soft top instead.

When the soft top is open, and regardless of whether this has been done manually or by a power system, the TT Roadster owner has a tonneau cover which can be spread out and secured over it. Other solutions such as automatically opening and closing sheet-metal covers, were discarded as too complex and space-wasting. Instead, the Roadster has the most welcome luggage capacity of 210 litres.

Härdl: "We wanted to stay with a classic solution, and therefore the soft top is not lined and the tonneau cover has to be attached by hand. But the rear window in the soft top is made of glass – an essentially modern and functional requirement."

Technical

But whether open or closed, the Ingolstadt-based Audi company has created a most remarkable new model in the shape of its TT Roadster, and one that will add a healthy impetus to the open-car market.

With the two versions of the TT, Audi has opened up a new chapter in the history of the sports car – not only by virtue of the car's unique appearance but also because the TT Coupé and TT Roadster demonstrate how design and technology, if brought together at a sufficiently early stage, do not necessarily have to conflict with one another.

On the contrary, the designers have here, in close cooperation with the engineers and technicians, produced one of those rare gems of the automobile world that make the jump from one-off creation to volume production vehicle without any compromises. Since this principle has functioned so well, we have every reason to hope that Ingolstadt teams will give us many more cars that pursue the same successful course as the TT. One thing is certain: the Audi board of management came, saw and liked this exceptional car – and its members know a good product when they see one!

Coupé and Roadster profit from every safety feature that can currently be incorporated into a modern passenger car, and have naturally passed all the relevant crash tests with flying colours.

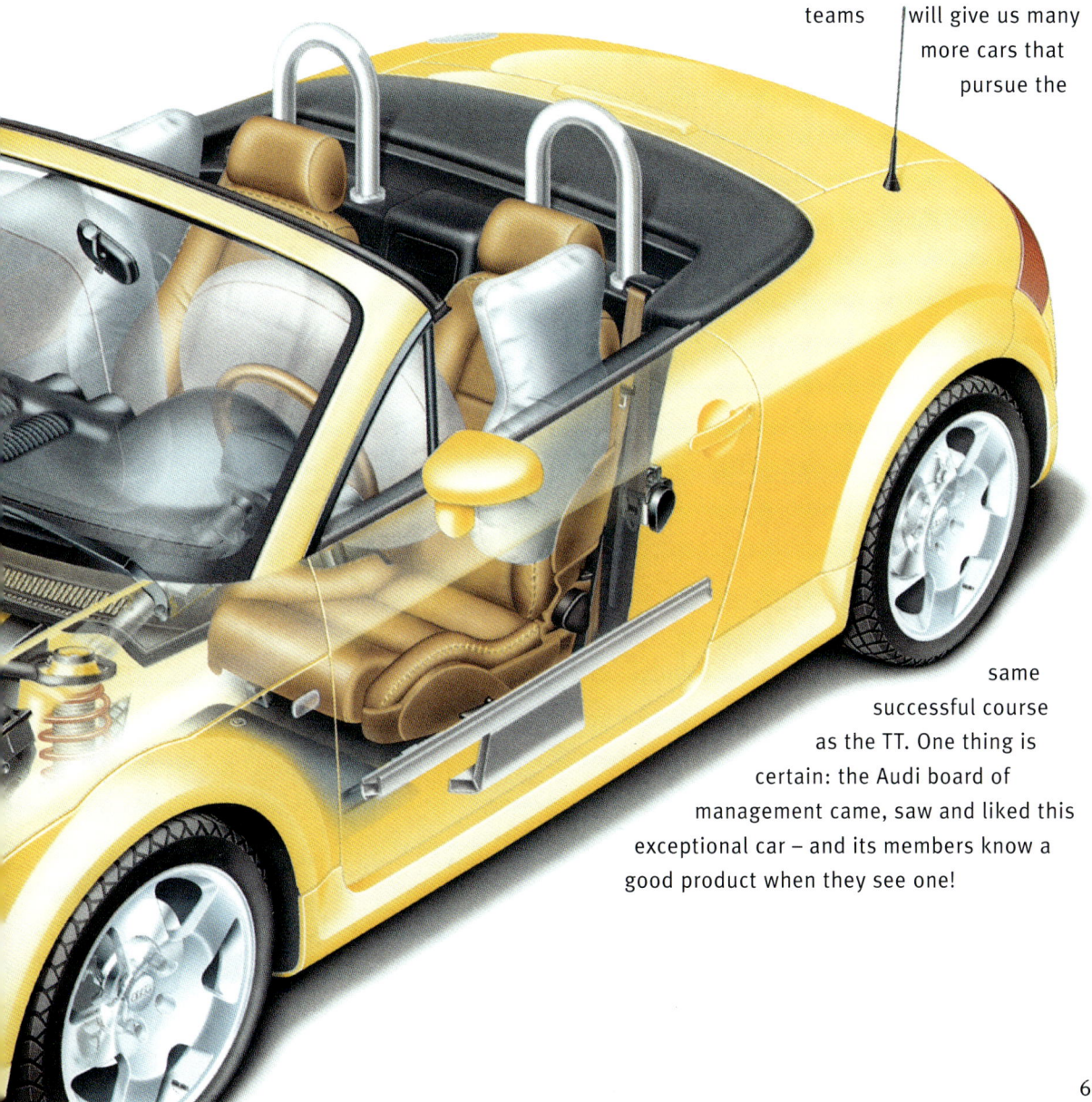

P R O D

U C T I O N

The commuter
The TT is always on the move

After the bare bodyshells manufactured in Ingolstadt have travelled to Győr overnight, they are unloaded from the enclosed rail vans in which they make the journey.

So that the new TT can be supplied to customer's order, each car is allocated its own build specification at the Győr plant.

One of the first production stages is to remove the doors, so that subsequent work inside the car is simplified.

THE TT IS THE FIRST AUDI to be built in two separate factories. With the aid of German Rail it commutes to and fro between the main plant in Bavaria and the Hungarian factory in Győr.

There were various reasons for this unusual procedure: first of all, the ultra-modern plant in Hungary already employs highly skilled personnel to assemble engines for the A3 and the TT.

Secondly, the Hungarian Government has declared the industrial zone to be duty-free, with worthwhile tax concessions that make car assembly there extremely interesting for Audi, aided by the excellent logistics laid on by the railway companies concerned.

Both the TT Coupé and the Roadster start life in Ingolstadt, where the bodyshell is made. This is where the big presses and welding robots are situated, and last but not least the brand-new paint shop, built at an investment of 500 million German Marks, where the successive coatings and the paint finish are applied to the body-in-white.

On completion, the bodies are loaded into enclosed rail freight cars and shipped to Hungary overnight, at a time when the railways have ample capacity for such movements to take place.

An ergonomically efficient, offset workplace layout is used for final assembly of the doors after they have been removed from the body.

At this stage, various members of the Audi workforce, which numbers 3,500 in all at this plant, start the final assembly procedures.

Engines come from elsewhere in the same plant – just across the street, one might say – but the remaining parts, from the suspension to the windows, are obtained from suppliers in many parts of the world. The parts are first grouped together into sets in Ingolstadt, then delivered to Győr, also by train.

After assembly, the cars are subjected to a thorough and detailed inspection routine, then board the train again for the journey back to Ingolstadt, where in due course they will be delivered to their proud owners.

A high standard of craftsmanship is needed for perfect assembly of the Coupé and Roadster dash panels – only after this pre-assembly stage is the complete cockpit module inserted into the car.

Production

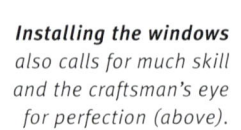

Installing the windows also calls for much skill and the craftsman's eye for perfection (above).

Work on the underside of the new TT becomes so much easier when it passes above the employees' heads on a suspended conveyor (top left).

The "marriage" is the time-honoured term used in the automobile industry for the moment when the engine and body are brought together (top right).

The marriage is consummated, so to speak, and detailed assembly work on the new TT can now begin.

Production

The marriage takes place in Hungary

The front-end module too is pre-assembled to one side of the main vehicle line, before being bolted to the bodyshell as a single, complete unit.

A special handling device moves the wheels up to the car and tightens all five wheel studs at the same time to the specific torque.

To minimise the risk *of damage, the finished doors are returned to the body for installation at the last possible moment.*

The final work stages *are mainly devoted to checking for correct operation – have the employees on the assembly line performed every task flawlessly?*

Now it's time to check *wheel alignment – toe-in and camber are measured and corrected if necessary.*

Production

Inspection – then the return journey to Ingolstadt

The TT encounters
its first rain shower in an ingeniously designed climatic test chamber – to make sure, for instance, that all the seals have been perfectly fitted.

One last glance
at the paint finish, while a colleague makes the car ready for despatch – and another new TT is ready to delight its owner.

A P P E**TT** A

R A N C E

No doubt the circular shapes of the TT influenced the design of the round exhibition stand at the Mondiale de l'Automobile, but they weren't the only reason why a million visitors wanted to stroke the TT's wheel arches.

A look back at Paris
A TT is a TT – and an apple is a "pomme"

When you stroll through a motor exhibition, you don't just admire the stands, take in the lighting displays and watch the hostesses as they give out hundreds of information brochures and lapel pins but still manage to keep smiling. You also sense that behind each company's presentation there is a well thought-out concept designed to reinforce its own particular message by the way it is built up and how it is conveyed.

So it comes as no surprise that the communication concept for the Paris International Motor Show in October 1998 was defined as a "Challenge to the Conventional" and as a "Charming Provocation".

Despite this challenging phrase, however, it was clear that the concept was based on Audi's close association with innovative technology and simple, uncluttered design. This was reflected in the slogan for the one hundredth *Mondiale de l' Automobile:* "Pure Audi" (the connoisseur of wine and spirits might say "Audi neat"!), a slogan that stands for a clear and consistent stance – especially in the engineering and design areas.

And what better model to represent this approach than the new TT?

Logically, therefore, Audi's stand at the Paris show was dominated by the TT coupé: no fewer than three in a clear geometrical formation, forming the centre of the Audi stand. Naturally, the slogan also exerted a dominant influence on the rest of Audi's presentation, because the clear lines of the TT and its resulting "presence" spoke for themselves. There was no need for further explanation or interpretation – a TT is a TT.

Logically enough, these were the only two letters that appeared on the car. Consistent with this approach, the Avant models were adorned with the word "Avant" and the A8 appeared as the "A8". Unsurprisingly perhaps, a wall was labelled "le mur".

Everything is what it is. This assessment attracted a lot of attention to the TT and the company that created it. Which in turn ensured that the name Audi was no longer thought of in the public mind as interchangeable with every other brand. The TT was an impressive visual embodiment of a message that conveyed the Audi outlook: clear, consistent, straight down the line, authentic.

However, in parallel with this bulk presentation of the new TT, Audi seized the opportunity of conveying the sporty character of the car with a novel video installation as well: a continuous ring of screens within the circular exhibition stand allowed the new coupé's dynamism to be demonstrated. In addition, the stand was used as a technical gallery to supply a concentrated account of the engineering that goes into the brand with the four rings.

Shown in the USA
The TT – or 100% Audi

Wherever you looked, everything in Detroit had to be one hundred percent in character. No wonder visitors to the exhibition stormed on to the stand and took all the bags and T-shirts they could get their hands on.

WHEREAS THE STAND AT THE PARIS MOTOR SHOW had been based on the circular forms of the TT and its wheel arches, the introductory slogan for the Detroit Motor Show in January 1999 was the expressive "100 % Audi".

The Audi exhibition stand at the Detroit Motor Show was overshadowed by a symbolic banked curve, on the sloping surfaces of which three TT Coupés seemed to float above the visitors' heads.

This presentation was supported by a sophisticated video installation that emphasised the dynamism of the banked curve: 100 % sporting performance plus 100 % aesthetic appeal. Concepts that match the TT just perfectly. In fact, the list is almost endless: 100 % design, 100 % consistency, 100 % personality …

Not forgetting what was actually the most important factor for many of the designers and engineers: 100 % passion.

This message was extended to the entire exhibition stand, and to the T-shirts, bags and give-aways. Wherever you looked, this was the message you saw. No wonder that the T-shirts and bags soon became something of a status symbol in Detroit – who doesn't enjoy being associated with 100 % passion or 100 % beauty?

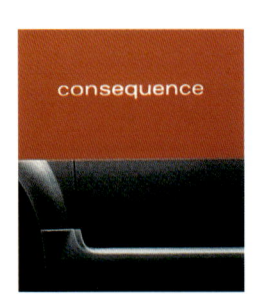

82 | 83

The overhead panels *represent the banked curves of one of the classic racetracks of the 1930s, with the TT Coupé as a model that became a classic as soon as it had been shown to the public.*

TT Appearance

So sieht Adrenalin aus.

Und hier entsteht es.   Audi TT. Driven by instinct.

Audi
Vorsprung durch Technik

Appearance TT

Promotion

With emotion in the forefront

By Jürgen Lewandowski

THERE ARE OF COURSE SIGNIFICANT MOMENTS in the lives and times of advertising agencies and their employees. For example, being invited to the city of Ingolstadt, Germany, for a sneak preview of a truly captivating Coupé and a most remarkable Roadster. After a lengthy preamble outlining the philosophy behind the cars, it is of course even more of a thrill to pass through the factory gates with a contract in one's pocket to dream up some brilliant advertising worthy of these exceptional vehicles.

For tasks of this kind, the Audi Agency Network (AAN) has been set up, with five advertising agencies in Germany, Great Britain, France, Spain and Italy as its members. These agencies are commissioned whenever a new model is under development, and of course receive their first briefing in plenty of time – two years before the actual market launch.

Before this first meeting with the creative heads of the advertising agencies takes place, the manufacturer's own marketing department has of course held numerous discussions with the stylists and engineers, and taken careful note of the concepts underlying their design and technical decisions. At these meetings, the product philosophy is defined, and the first essentials for marketing and advertising the new car materialise.

It was obvious from the outset that sports cars too were encountering a change of public values, and indeed that it was likely to affect them more than most other types of car. Their fascination no longer stems from sheer brute force or martial presence on the road.

Aggression is distinctly out these days, but the resulting change of values has revealed the power of other emotions instead. As the publicity people put it so neatly: "Without emotion, life surely isn't worth living. So let's forget sheer common-sense just occasionally and enjoy a bit more fun in life!"

In addition to this strong emotional element, the TT Coupé and its open-topped counterpart both make a second clear statement: here I am, a true sports car, a sports car from AUDI! This is the technical-competence company, the manufacturer that has always been technologically led. This circumstances makes the TT a no-compromises, thoroughbred sports car, capable of redefining the seminal fascination of this type of car and communicating this experience to those who ride in it and drive it. In a word: the authentic, close-to-the-skin experience of true active driving.

With all this in mind, the urge to present the TT Coupé and TT Roadster to the public as pure "designer cars" in the modern sense of the term was a strong one. Yet Herbert Flandörfer, member of the AUDI board of management for marketing, declares firmly that "we never discussed presenting the TT with special emphasis on design – this is an aspect that speaks for itself, and didn't need any extra emphasis from us."

In fact, the basic elements of the TT's market presentation were soon defined: the car is the centre of attention, no people need to be shown to illustrate its position and its form and technical features can be allowed to speak for themselves. It is an authentic sports car capable of demonstrating its merits on the great roads of the world.

Adrenaline:
could be defined as a pure kind of advertising aimed at arousing the curiosity.

The authentic active driving experience

Instinct, passion and excitement: a far from everyday combination of emotions generated by a highly emotive, desirable object. Surely these words ought to end in "TT"? Some slight modifications to the German language and the job was done.

The true character of the TT called for the various versions' power outputs to be revised upwards. The original plan for a basic car developing 150 bhp would not have achieved the outstanding performance that the planners in Ingolstadt had in mind. The top model was therefore boosted to 225 bhp, which also served the marketing function of distinguishing it more clearly from the most potent S versions in the A3 and A4 model lines.

Allied to the desire to communicate more emotion, the direction which an authentic TT for the active driver had to take was now clear. The result has proved to be a car of amazingly individual character. Thanks to AUDI's sheer technical competence, it represents an emotional experience and a seldom paralleled object of desire.

Nor is the TT's emotive punch dependent on nostalgia for times past or design echoes from bygone eras. It conveys the values associated with the true sports car and the authentic active driving experience in a thoroughly modern way.

The months passed, and executives from the Audi Agency Network met regularly to shape their concept and interpret the manufacturer's own mental picture of the car. From the guiding principles discussed two years before the TT's scheduled appearance, a precise briefing for the desired advertising campaigns in print and on TV emerged in the course of the next twelve months.

After a further four weeks, the team was ready to present the agencies' initial outlines – always an exciting moment, since from this meeting onwards the direction that advertising will take is more or less finalised. These decisions have to be transformed into reality within a period of two to three months, yet there is always a strong element of instinctive choice involved. A good slogan or effective artwork inspires a feeling of excitement somewhere deep down in the "pit of the stomach", and tells us quite unmistakably: "This is it!"

For the TT, the crucial slogan that summed up the entire campaign was soon found:

Audi TT – driven by instinct.

What did this simple sentence tell us? Surely that the rational principles we apply to run our lives today have tended to suppress something that's vital to the essential elements of life: the world of feelings and emotions or, if we go back to the genuine roots, of human instincts. The key message of the campaign was found, with the AUDI TT as its symbol.

Once again, some months elapsed as the layout, the choice of colours and the pictorial language were developed to suit the tenor of this campaign: reduced to essentials, with no superfluous ornament, powerful, primeval – almost elemental, yet never without charm and therefore with no bombast or hero-worship. What better way to symbolise the AUDI marque too: provocative, emotionally stimulating, but never less than intelligent and with the very slight hint of irony that comes with true self-awareness.

Appearance

The campaign and its "flavour" had to be new, refreshing, almost avant-garde in style. Three to four months before the TT presentation, it was shown in fully-developed form to the AUDI board of management, which strongly approved of the concept of presenting the TT in this combination of purist but emotional forms.

The campaign was launched with such keywords as adrenaline, egoism and change well to the fore – pure and progressive, awakening the most powerful curiosity. After the first advertisements had drawn initial attention to the TT, the German language was mildly but determinedly distorted to attach the model letters to a series of highly emotive concepts: instincTT, lusTT etc.

The advertising campaign harboured at least one major surprise: the unforgettable Christmastide image of a whole fleet of TT Coupés driving through the square in front of the Chicago Stock Exchange. Another delightful idea was the highly selective snowflake, which examined all the available vehicles most critically before deigning to alight on the TT.

TT Roadster advertising, logically, is closely linked to that for the TT Coupé, with the same general mood, similar claims and if anything still more emotive visuals, the implication being that this stimulating form of driving can be even more fun in an open car.

As an AUDI executive put it: advertising campaigns should be more fun. They should inspire empathy and communicate visual pleasure at the highest level. A glance at the TT advertising confirms that this objective has certainly been reached.

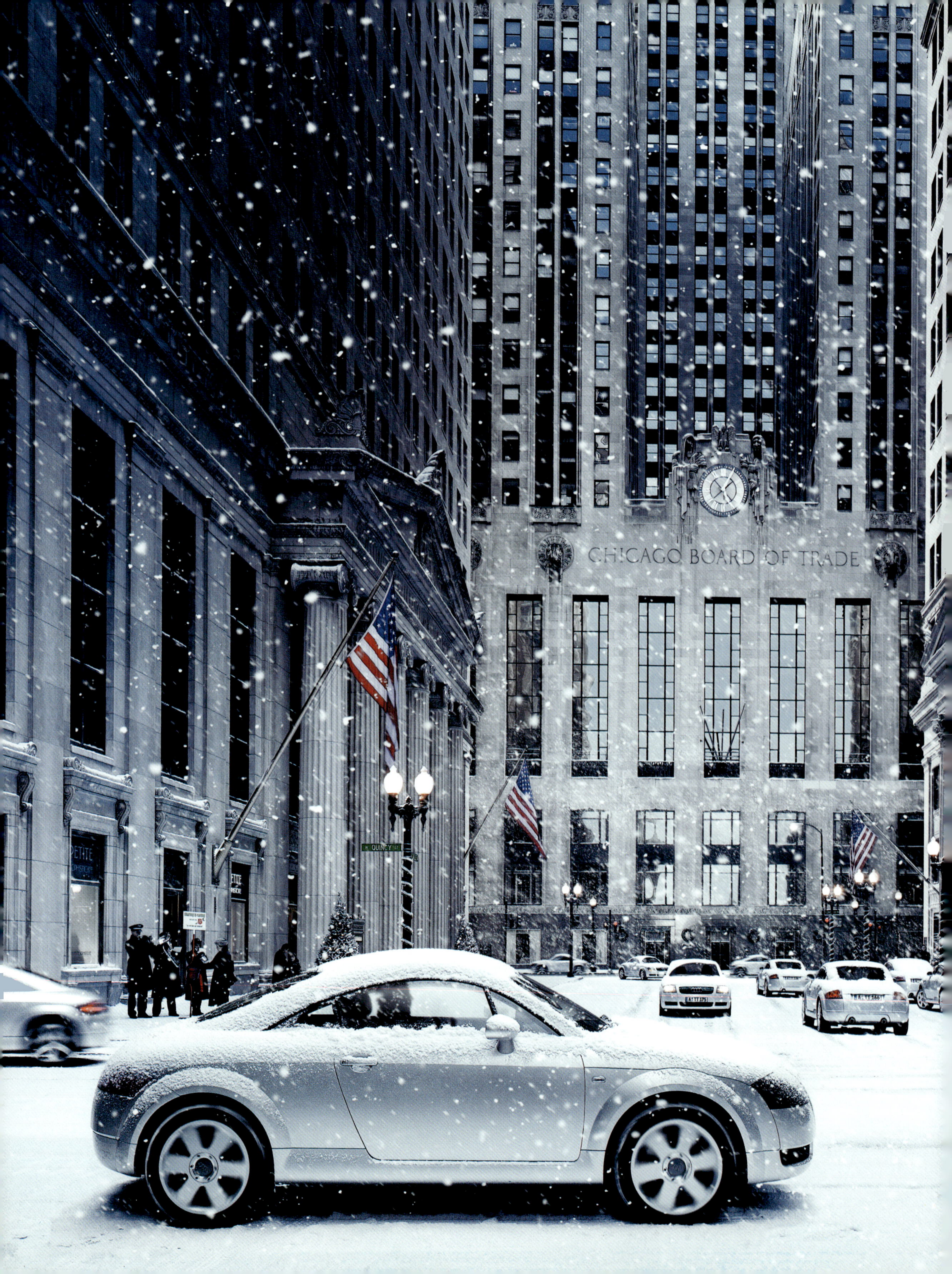
CHICAGO BOARD OF TRADE

The big surprise for Christmas 1998: *a group of Audi TT Coupés on the snowbound streets in front of the Chicago Stock Exchange. All of them, naturally, have quattro four-wheel drive to cope succesfully with this kind of weather.*

TT Appearance

I C E L A N

D

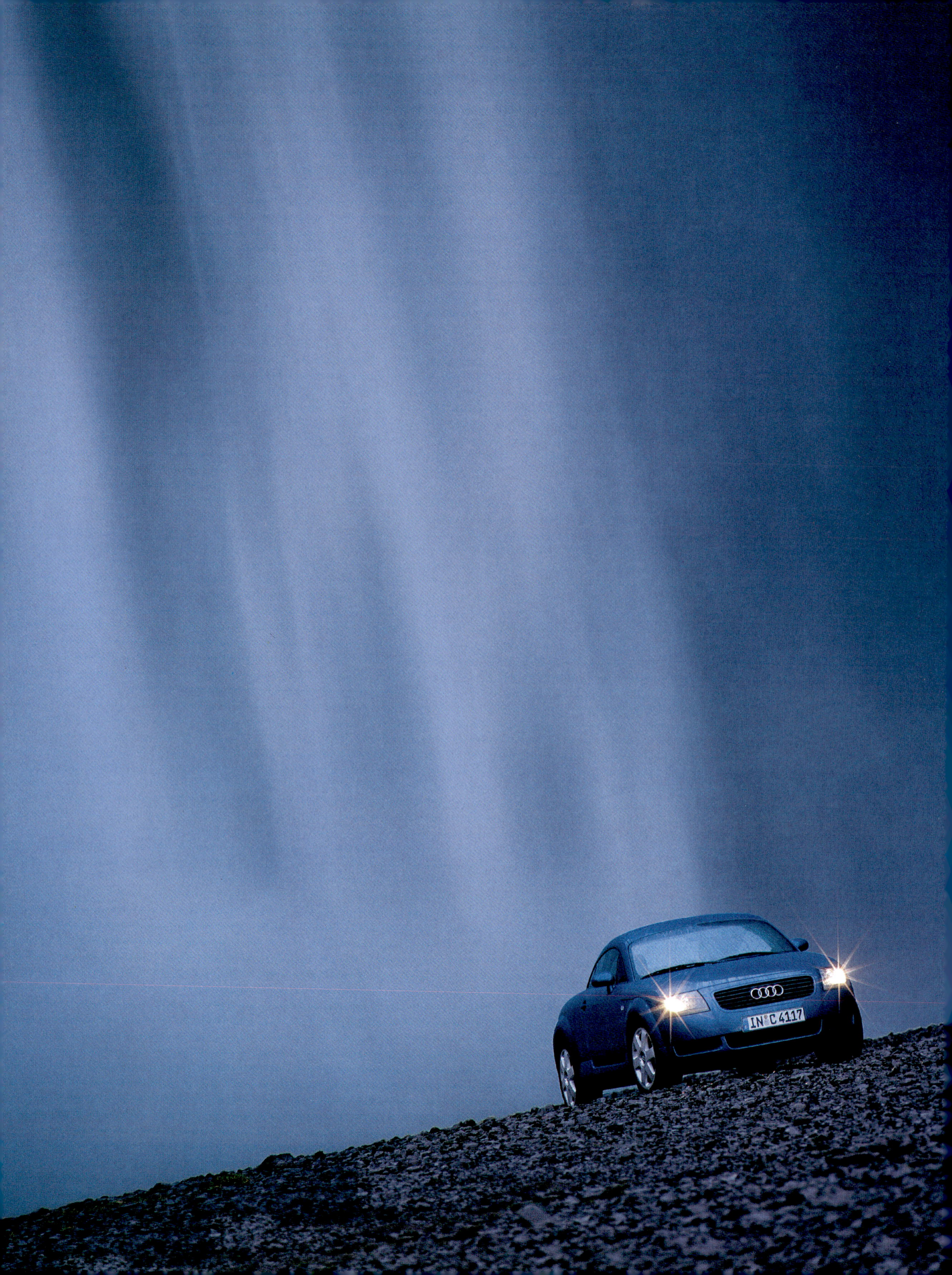
IN C 4117

Iceland

The making-of-story of the introductory photos

by Herbert Völker

THIS IS ALSO THE STORY OF LONG PERIODS spent sitting in the car, waiting and reading. If you sit in the car for a long time in Iceland, you will like to read Icelandic books, not just out of politeness. Icelandic literature, both old and new, is sensational, and so there are enough translations into languages which you can understand. Of course, people's names are not translated, as everywhere else in the world.

The main character in my first book was called Hrafnkel, and you can guess the problems which a reader has with a hero called Hrafnkel.

Even if you are quite practised in reading and no longer move your lips, you still come to a point about three times on every page where you brake to a stop, change down from fifth gear and then slowly drive over it:

H-raf-n-kel.

It is less of a problem that he took a wife called Oddbjörg Skjödolfsdottir. You can imagine him tenderly calling her Otti, but what does she call him?

Not Hrafnkel, sweetheart?

So there we sat during the long Icelandic evenings and discussed the matter with Hanna, our guide. Originally, we were supposed to be having a male guide, but a happy accident kept him in the capital city and sent us this angel.

When a team otherwise consisting of men is in the wilderness, it is quite useful if they are all slightly in love in a nice way. It is in the interest of consideration and punctuality and everybody going over the hill to pee.

So I ask Hanna: "Hrafnkel. Is it pronounced as it is written? So nerve-shatteringly?"

"No, it is quite simple" says Hanna. "In Icelandic, an "f" is pronounced like a "p" and in "-kel", there is an invisible "j" and an invisible "t", so it sounds like "-kjetl". And the "H" at the beginning is like hard breathing-out. So we say Hrabnkyetl."

So that had solved that. A nice name. For the TT, Iceland was the invention of Peter Vann.

So let us briefly address the person of Peter Vann. Can anybody be called Vann? It sounds as if a young man had a name which was far too long, like they have in dark valleys, and wanted to go to Paris and be a popstar. A manager looked at him for a long time and said with a sigh: "From now on, you will be called Vann".

That was roughly what happened. The boy from the depths of Switzerland served a proper appenticeship as a photographer to please his father, was allowed to go to drama school as a reward, turned out to be a pop singer, but only in Switzerland, where everything closed at nine o'clock then. So he went to Paris, was dicovered by Adamo's and Cliff Richard's producer, abbreviated to Vann and sent into battle with Johnny Halliday, who was just as good-looking as Peter, maybe a tad better. The rest is history.

The anti-postcard
The waterfalls of Skügar are one of the most spectacular tourist sights in the south of Iceland. So it is to be feared that the morif will be reduced to a postcard-idyll. Peter Vann shows how to avoid this risk.

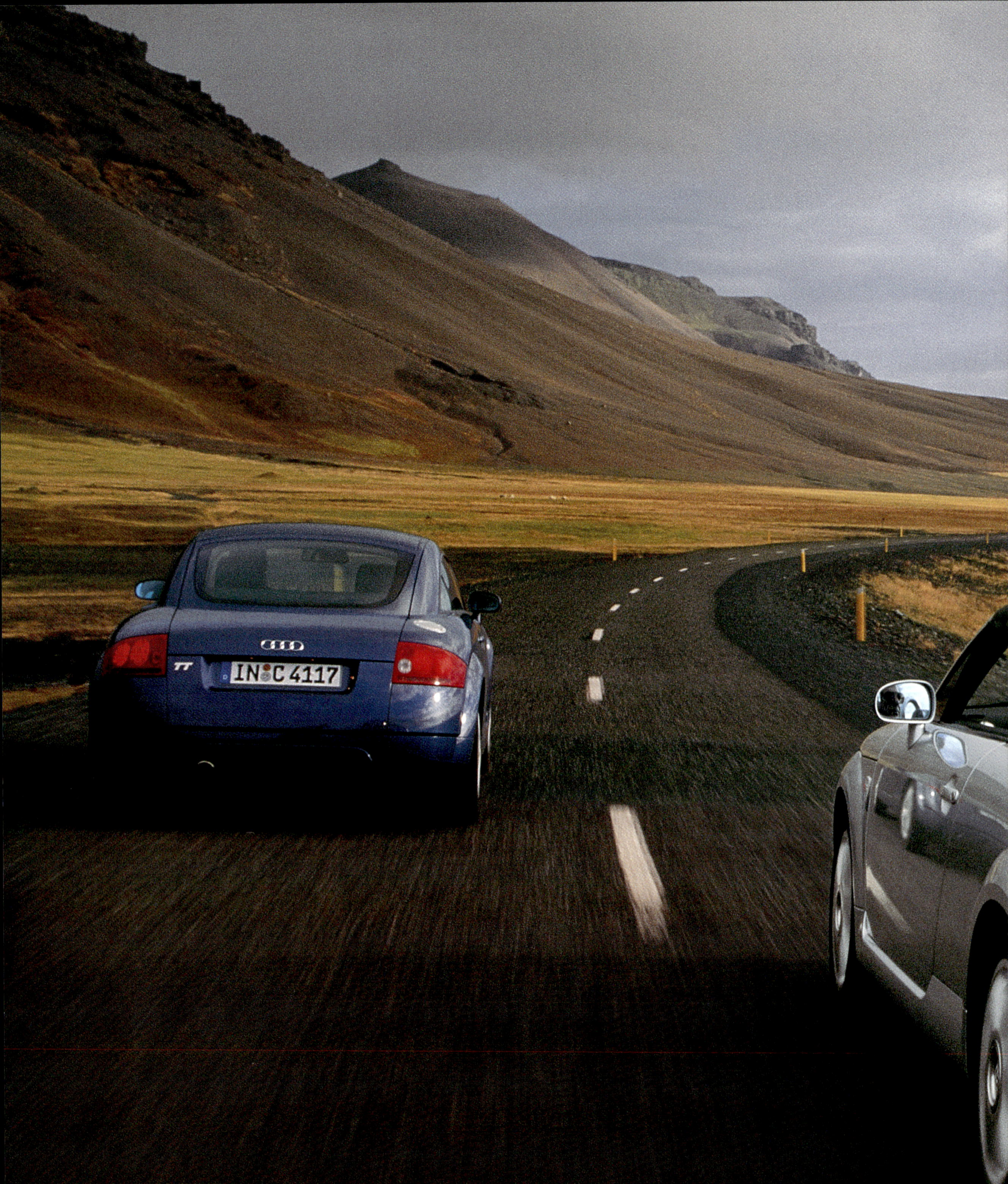
TT
IN C 4117

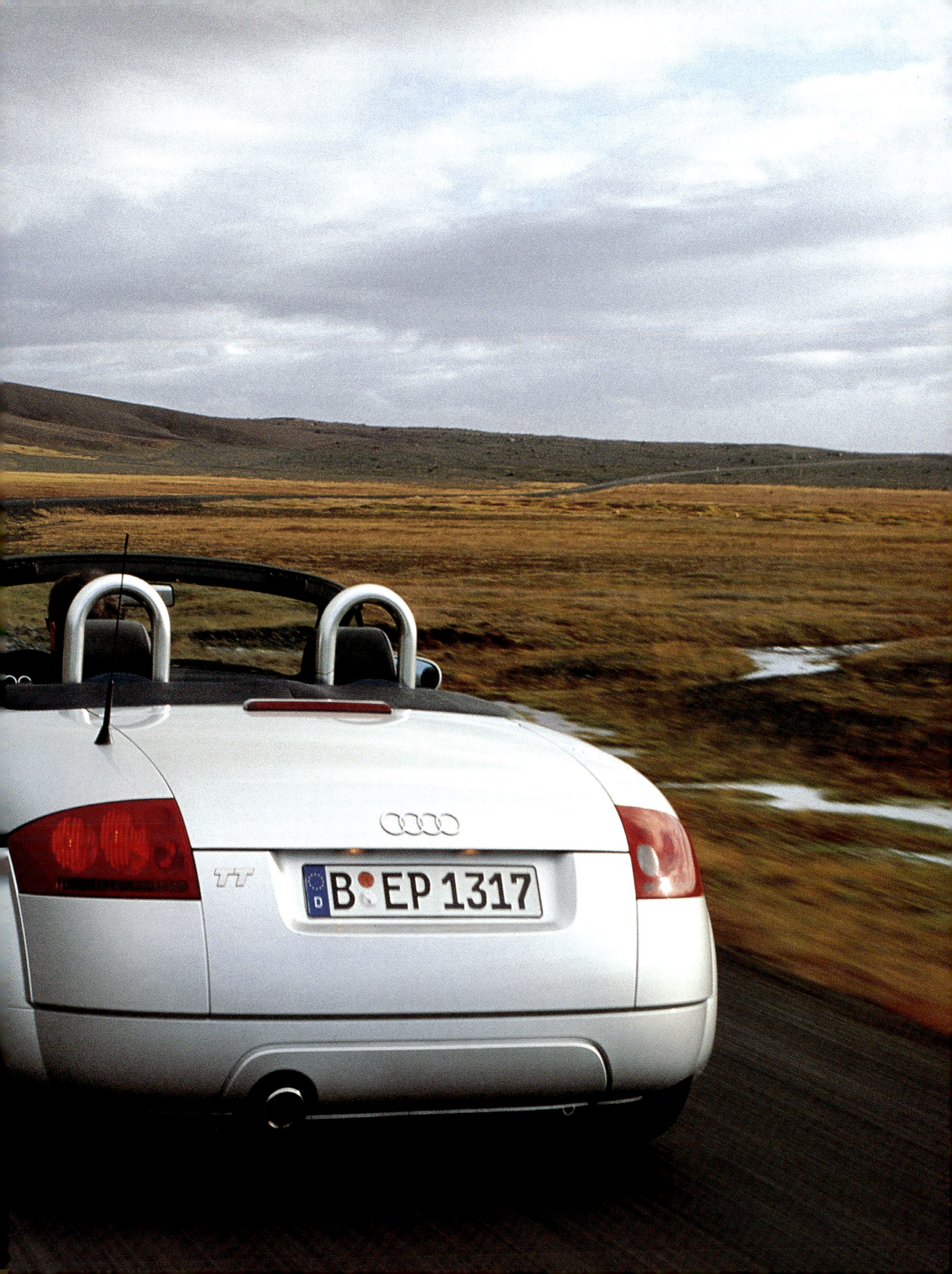
TT
B EP 1317

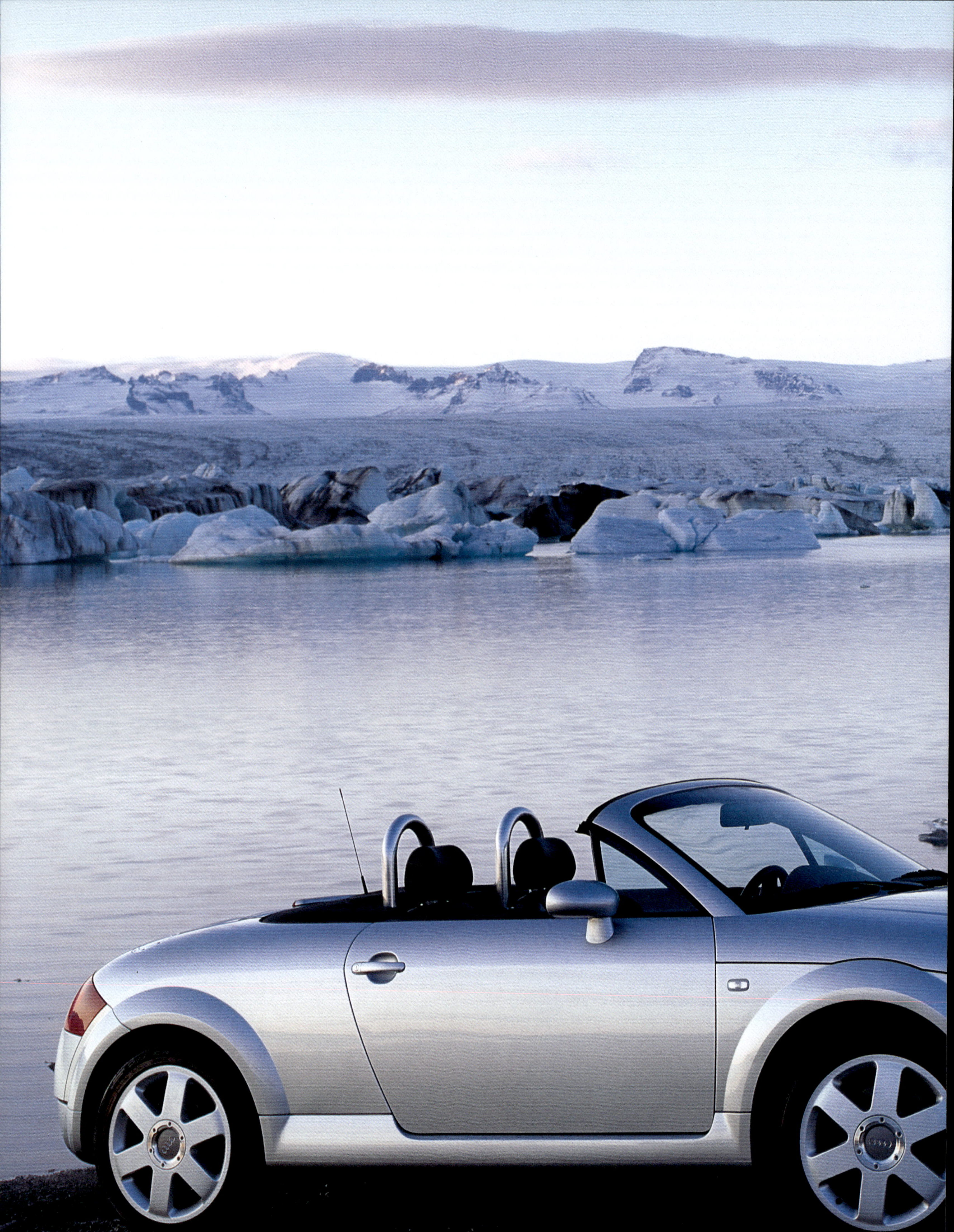

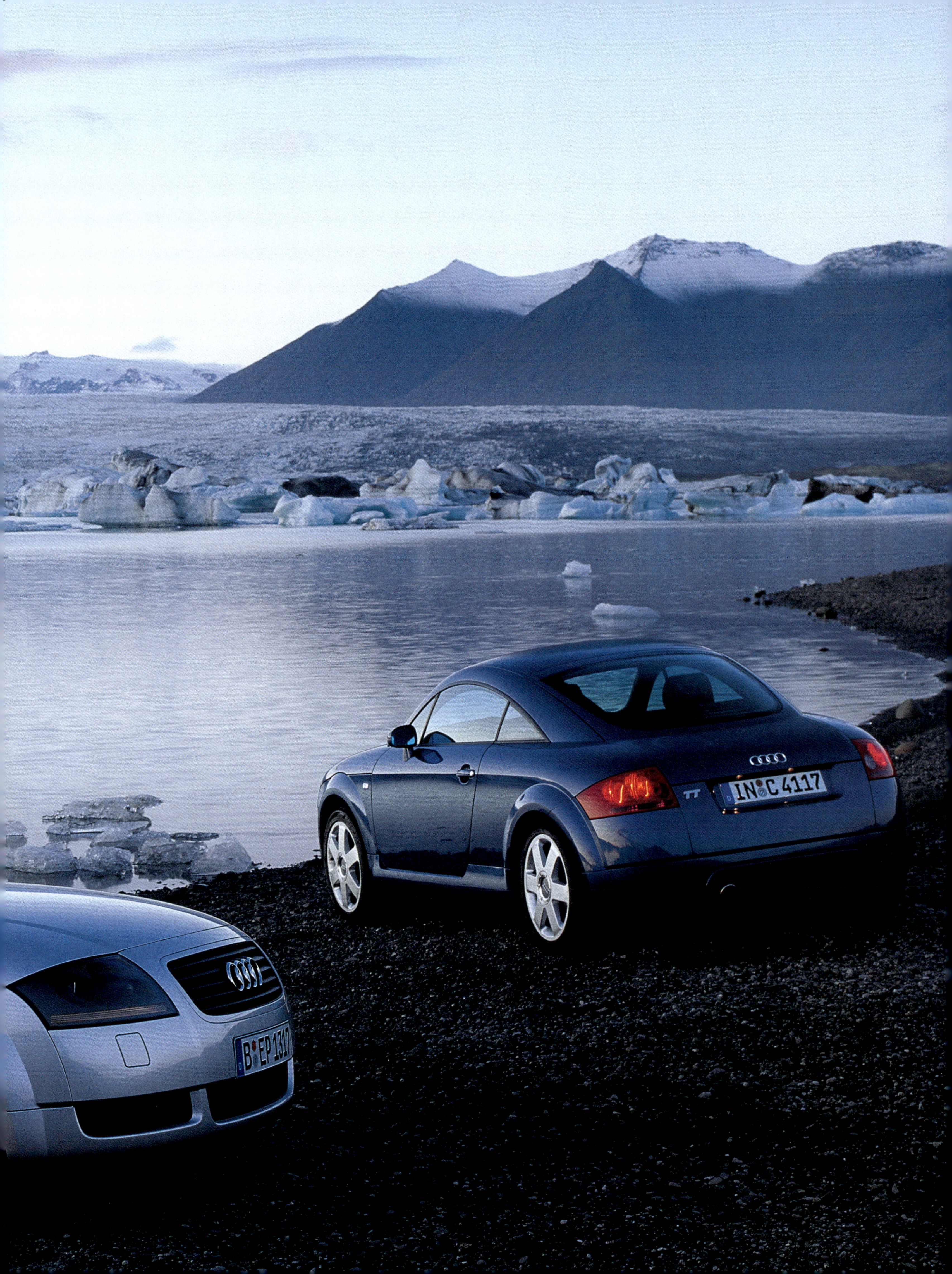
TT
IN C 4117

The location? Initially secret

The graphics
This is probably what Peter Vann means when he talks about the graphic nature of both the Icelandic countryside and Audi design (incidentally, the hardtop suits the roadster beautifully).

A woman put him back on his feet and he finaly became a photographer. He kept the practical name of Vann.

Vann is one of the few photographers who cross over between advertising and reporting. There are so few because pay is four times higher in advertising than for "editorial stuff" and then nobody finds their way back.

But just as he was experiencing his greatest successes as an international advertising Zampano, with a stylish assistant and gazelles all around him like in the Serengeti, he got a longing for the simple life and the balanced message.

So now and then he takes the virtues of best advertising photography (bold and eye-catching, highly sensitive to location, more time, more money) back to the other side (magazine photography) and lets the man of feeling, which he has always been, get on the cart. The resulting photographic style is then: Peter Vann.

Vann sometimes does secret campaigns for automotive companies, who are planning their advertising programmes with a run-up of many months or preparing their press material. This work is then so top-secret that Peter covers all the traces of his trip until he sometimes cannot find himself either. This is called an identity crisis.

It is only a fair penalty for his bad habit of stringing along even his best friends. He rings up and talks about the weather in England, for example, while he is sitting in a tavern in Turin and waiting for Giugiaro to finally hammer the last nail into the new Bugatti.
In the trade, this is called: CONFIDENTIALITY.

For understandable reasons, he predominantly takes photographs in places which are beautiful and warm and where there are not thousands of people about. Of course, for this type of work, he has someone from Corporate Security with him, and as soon as any person appears, they throw a coat over the car and will not let Peter continue work until the potential spy has gone. So he does not do these jobs in Central Europe very often but prefers Arizona or Morocco. Companies take this in their stride. They are already accustomed to extreme locations for their test drives and also prefer the sun of Mesa Verde on their cars to a breath of Gelsenkirchen.

So initially, he went on his own to look for a location for the new Audi. And secretly. We at home could do no more than guess where the blazing rays of the exotic sun on the swelling body of a TT Roadster would soon be producing photographic highlights. At last he returned.

Iceland, he said, Iceland in October.

Initially, Peter knew nothing about Iceland. It was just an idea – he could just as easily have thought of Uzbekistan. But it was Iceland he thought of, and this vague, fragile idea had then been confirmed during location-making. The word is not my invention – all photographers say "location-making".

Iceland

Iceland

The plastics.
A low structured background allows sculpture to stand out, emphasises the Roadster's own features.

It was a journey from October to January

Federal Highway 1
One sole highway encircles the island, the size of which we southerners often do not really understand. More than 100,000 sq.km – Switzerland, for example, would fit in there two-and-a-half times.

Iceland

A photographer whom we like to watch at work

It means looking for good photo places in a country you don't know. So you take along a clever local to help you look.

How to envisage the special character that Peter Vann expected? A certain type of landscape? A certain temperature of light? Icebergs, glaciers, waterfalls, bald hills?

He says that it had to be seen and felt. It could not be talked about. Just as his photographic style could not be explained. Previously, he mumbled something about Protestant purism, but that was the end of the line.

Purism – that is not a style, is it?

"Oh, style" says Peter Vann, "a photographer finds style like a wrapped present under the Christmas tree. You unpack it and have got a good or bad style. For the rest of your life, there are only changes in circumstances or nuances."

In Iceland, it is always three months colder than in Central Europe. So it was a journey from October to January. Vann's planning is very lean. Basically, he only needs himself and the car to be photographed.

Nevertheless, he does not exactly travel alone. What has to be taken is: a second car for photographing, to be on the safe side. The assistant. The scout (as already mentioned, it was a scoutess, thank heavens). Two men from Audi security. The captain for the car transporter. The lady from Iceland's environmental protection agency who appeared on occasions (strict habits, thank heavens again).

The cook.

From one cook upwards, you need a kitchen bus. Plus a driver for the kitchen bus. This means a mechanic = man of all trades = assistant of transport captain. Plus an accompanying journalist. Even a TV team was scheduled to join in towards the end. So, despite all leanness, you suddenly have a transporter, a kitchen bus, a photo jeep, a TV jeep, a scout jeep, a security jeep and a mobile journalist, plus, of course, the two Audis up on the transporter.

They must never be forgotten, otherwise everyone will be sitting in the kitchen bus, will have covered their tracks and won't be able to remember why.

But that is not what happened.

So it was Iceland. Before you can think about landscape and photographic motifs and the job, you first have to come to terms with being on a strange planet. You have no link to your normal life, it is simply too far away and it doesn't matter. This is a lonely island and nothing distracts you from this romantic fact. Your mobile phone works in Reykjavik but otherwise only at certain places in the country, and after the second day, you stop caring about them too. It was probably good to arrive in October when there are no tourists, who may possibly make everything a little more commonplace in the season.

A windy job.
From wind force 3 upwards, the long tube on the Hasselblad starts to tremble on the tripod. A miniature has to be used sometimes.

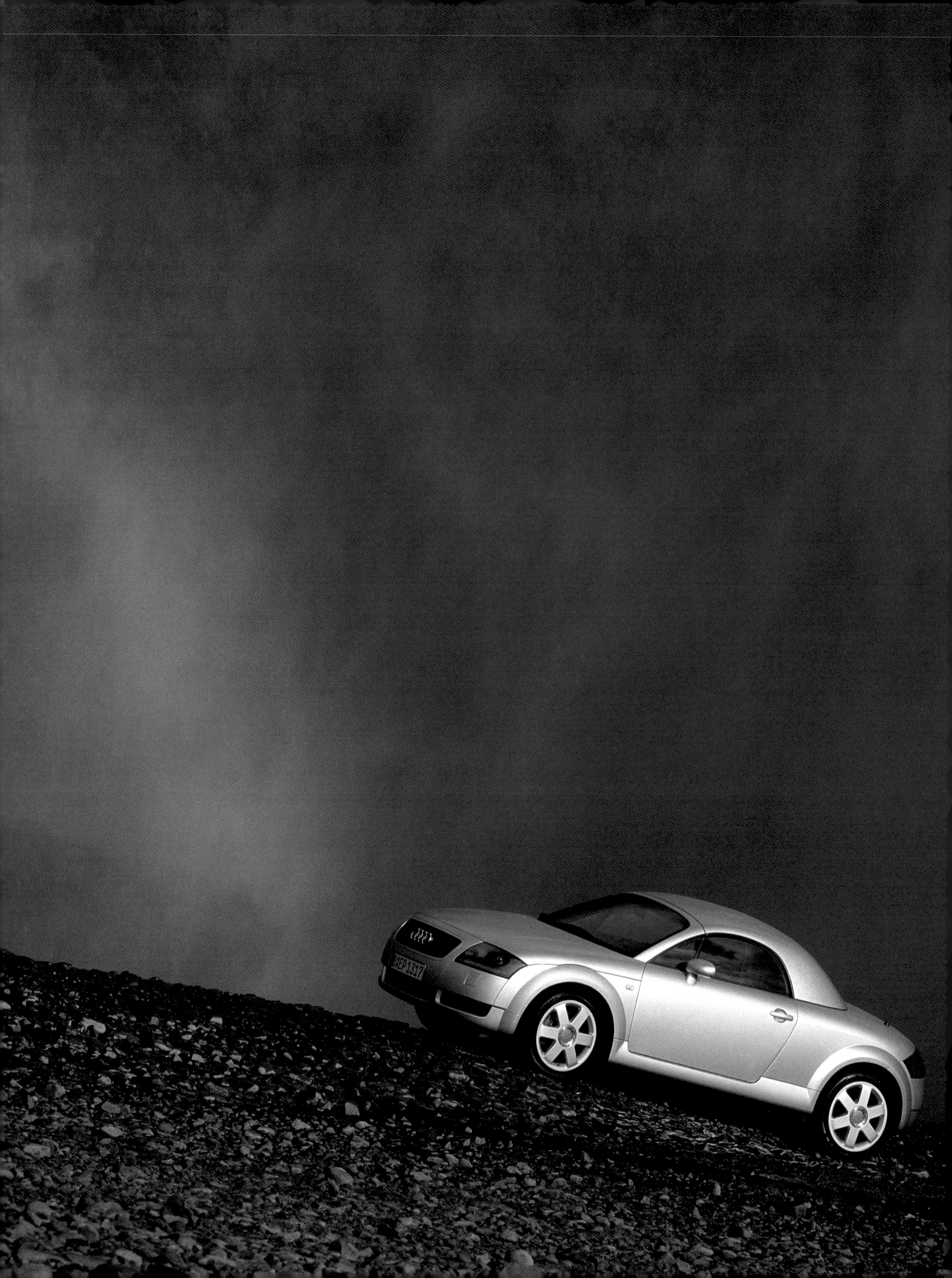
HEP 1317

The photographic subject always travels incognito.

Iceland

In the land below the glaciers, the rivers do as they please.

Iceland

Underwater adventure

Things can quickly become serious
Since the torrents of water from the mountains and glaciers continually seek new routes, bridges are pointless anyway, so they do not exist. Even good off-roaders have their limits. A securing system is called for and preferably an 8 x 8 drive. Meanwhile, the kitchen bus stays on the reasonably dry side. This is why everybody always found their way back safely.

TV on location.
For colleagues from RTL, the exotic photo production was also worth a shooting.

Anyway, the beauty of the strange planet hits you so hard in the stomach that your brain has trouble in catching up. Where has this sudden love of the bare and barren come from? It is like the fulfilling of a great longing – whatever may be behind such a longing.

So it is easy to love EVERYTHING here, right down to the dish of fish-liver oil which they give you for breakfast (not ONLY fish-liver oil, at any rate). And oh, the wonderful language. Not as goitrous as Danish, not as singsong as Swedish, not as Hungarian as Finnish, even more brittle than Norwegian – up here, the throaty and the guttural have been united.

From this exploratory mission in the summer, Peter Vann had brought polaroids of about ten locations, all in the south of the island (if he had wanted to use the whole Icelandic spectrum, it would have been a two-month expedition).

Location 1 is Crater Lake.

Lava edge, i.e. black, the lake Icelandic blue, the opposite slope a reserved red, as if the moss had gone rusty. Put a silver TT Roadster there, press the shutter, and it is almost unbearable.

So we are heading for this fantastic polaroid, already deep in the highlands, no people, no sheep, no nothing. Five hours' driving, and after the fifth hour, everything is shitty, Foggy, dull, a roaring gale, we battle against the rain like Doctor Zhivago.

We sit in our cars and stare at the patches of fog, which are changing up from second to third gear. ICELAND. PETER VANN'S IDEA.

Hanna knows the name of the lake.

Ljóttipollur, she says, that means the brave lake. It appeared in the 15th century after a series of volcanic eruptions. The Icelanders have a very precise history going back a thousand years. So this one wasted day does not really seem so important.

The rain eases. Peter has the Roadster unloaded, puts all his equipment in position, everything gets wet and clammy and awful, but at least someone has shown his colours. Work is being done here! The Roadster is leathered dry. But there are no colours and no depth and everything is a waste of time. Not a single picture. Although the kitchen bus did not make up to the crater edge, we find it back in the hinterland.

Please do not think it is easy to find an isolated kitchen bus deserted in the Icelandic highlands, but we manage it. Although we do not have a single picture taken, we have a cosy kitchen bus.

Our cook is called Stefan. He normally runs a fish restaurant in Reykjavik, but he has seen lots of road movies and so he loves to charter this bus and fill it with guests who deserve it.

Ten days,
a net production
of six major
motifs.

Iceland

A scout named Hanna

A woman
who went to university in Paris and can speak all languages, who loves the wilderness and never bends a blade of grass.

All good films made in Iceland were fed, warmed and dried in this bus. A decent kitchen bus is the mother of photography, is what I say.

We drove to the hostile crater again, packed everything up, tried the next location and then returned to the lake. Suddenly the colours were there, not completely but nevertheless there, and only miniature could be used, because the gale made the large tube of the Hasselblad tremble on the tripod, but it was okay.

From then on, it got better and better, and from the third day onwards, Iceland was a good friend of Peter Vann's TT Roadster production. In all honesty, it must be said, that Iceland could have been a disaster. It is simply much more risky than some pretty southern destination, especially in October.

In this country, which is two and a half times as big as Switzerland, there is only one single highway. It greases the contours of the island. Everything that takes place off this road can suddenly become an adventure. We were able to experience this to the full. Once, the Atlantic wanted to grab the little Roadster. It simply stuck out its greedy cold tongue – heaven forbid! Once, we would have had to abandon an outrageously expensive jeep (all cars in Iceland are outrageously expensive) to a river, if our transport captain hadn't been on the bank with an 8 x 8.

And of course Hanna. Hanna, our scout, is our blissful image of Iceland today.

The woman who went to university in Paris, can speak all languages, loves the wilderness and never bends a blade of grass. In the dark of winter, she has a cultural job in the capital.

She quickly made us respect the radical environmental concept with which the Icelanders conserve their unique country, and we took pleasure in brushing away the turning tracks of our cars in certain places, centimetres away from the lava rubble path.

We drove through the south of Iceland for ten days, with a net production of six major motifs. Two-thirds of the time, it can be said, were spent waiting at the location. Waiting for the light to become a bit different, to become just as Peter Vann wanted it.

We still had the kitchen bus.

Stefan cooked in the evenings too, when we found accommodation in small hotels or just former containers for road workers. In the highlands, there is practically nowhere to stay between October and May. Anyway, there was a sort of community house nearby, where parties are held in the summer, I assume, and the transporter captain had hot-air machines with him.

Iceland

The first job of the hot-air machines was to warm the red-wine bottles. Fortunately, we did not have Château Palmer '85, but original Icelandic supermarket wine, which takes thawing very well. The first bottle still tastes a bit of the north but things improve with the second one.

While we were waiting for our meal and long afterwards, we talked clever talk, which became cleverer and cleverer and ever more charming in light Icelandic fashion, depending on how brilliantly Viktor had held the red wine into the hot-air machine.

Anyway, one evening in the highlands, Peter Vann was in good form.

I asked: "Is there something special about Icelandic light?"

"It's northern light. At this time of the year, there is ten minutes' less sun every day, and midday light is replaced more and more by twilight. The rounder the earth, the faster the sun goes down, but you should check that, because I don't want to be thought an idiot. *(No danger of that, if "round" means the belly of the earth's diameter. i.e. equator = completely round. – Author's Note)* Be that as it may, you profit from this long twilight here. It is cold light and very dramatic light."

"What does "dramatic" mean?"

"It is a stimulating light for colours. There may only be very little light, but blades of grass suddenly begin to light up like glow-worms. It is also a threatening light, aggressive, uncannily animating light."

"What role do the colours of a car play under these circumstances?"

"Under difficult conditions, you are always on the safe side with silver. If we only had a red and a green car here, we could give up straight away ... although ... a classic Ferrari red would perhaps have to be tested first. But green or yellow – inconceivable."

"What are your favourite colours?"

"I have a weakness for grey. Grey shades, blue shades and black. These are the only colours I wear."

"Could there be a completely different car here? I mean – Iceland and the TT Roadster, is that a coincidence or did you think about it?"

"The fact that the Roadster is open does not play any part but the whole Audi design does. Nature here has a graphic structure, and this goes fantastically well with the way Audi portrays itself in design, and particularly in the TT. Nature helps me to express what I want to say. Nature becomes graphics, if it is seen properly. If it is approached wrongly, it is degraded to a postcard. That is the danger with all graphic backgrounds. The same applies to the lakes, icebergs, glaciers – they can be photographed well or badly. If you are not careful, they become postcards.

"Where is the difference between good and bad?"

"Whatever I say now would sound arrogant. It is a question of your personal way of doing things. So I am not afraid of working at places where a hundred photographers have worked before me – I simply do it differently somehow."

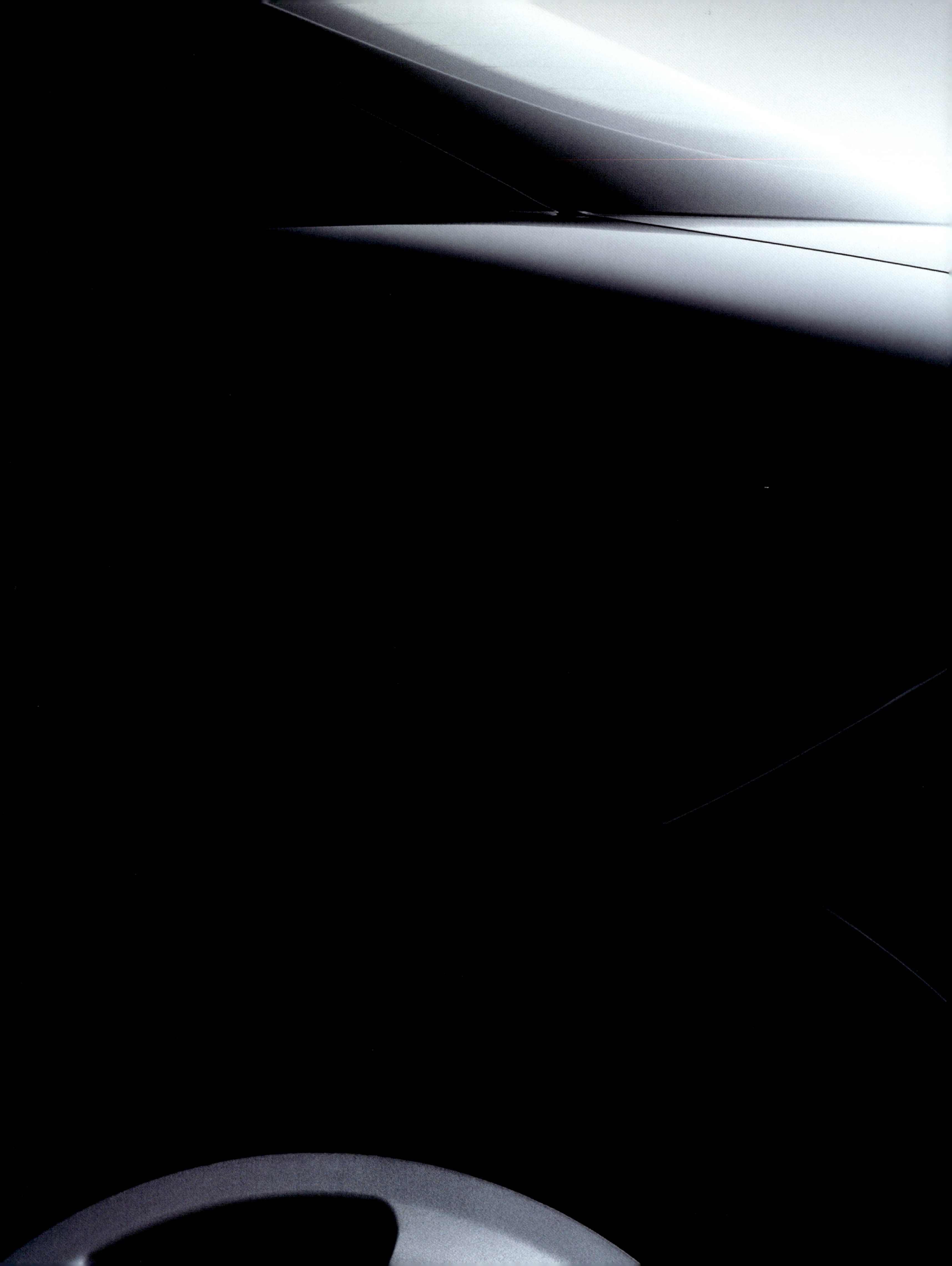

P A R I S

Paris

The Little Sparrow of Paris

The car that loves the city *by David Staretz*

THE PAVEMENT IS STILL WET WITH RAIN. The waiter from the café in the Rue de Turbigo presses a broom under the bulging awning. Touché! As if sound were running in the wrong direction, the flood of water sloshes down on the pavement – light coloured spray, wet trouser legs. Someone curses under his breath. A few forgotten car headlights throw reflections on the asphalt surface, scatter in the haze.

Tyres begin to leave patterns which dry onto the road. Sun sprinkles from a thousand drops. A black-and-white dog crosses the street with a clever look, snapping casually at a pigeon, because he is expected to. The first umbrellas are forgotten in cafés.

Paris is always a little like the cinema, everything seems to have a second level confirming the first. Even the careless, the incidental, is more intensive. Here the pigeons appear more select, the women more mysterious, the Eiffel Tower more incredible.

Down there stand the slim men from Tunisia, Zaire or Nigeria. They are still winding up their artificial birds, which have elsewhere long gone the way of all seasonal articles. They throw the flapping celluloid bodies with slovenly elegance. Surprising turbulence, grace of coincidence, dying flap on the ground. Little girls fetch the twitching plastic birds, mothers rush nervously after them. Ransoming instincts awake.

Intense life, an experimental set-up: "As soon as an object exceeds the critical mass, it emits attraction forces which are stronger than the centrifugal ones." Yes, higher physics is still a hit after all, as shown by the TT, even at a standstill.

The days of tiny letter-boxes in sports cars are over.
The TT is compatible to many a conceptual objet d'art (often bulky!), and the smart lid drops into place over it with exciting exactness.

Here, in the liveliness of this city, the TT appears so particularly appropriate and especially refreshing, because the city suffers dramatically from the multitude of ugly small cars.

Most of them look like old trainers and have nothing in common with great architecture. The TT has a completely different approach – it is emotionally charged but externally unmoved.

An example occurs to me, a black-and-white photo which Jim Rakete took of Bruce Springsteen. It was taken in Berlin, but that doesn't matter.

Content of the photo – Bruce is driving an unadornedly open, credibily dirty Porsche Speedster (the James Dean model) across a square. Nothing else. But there is not too much and not too little, this picture easily masters the presence of the star-in-museum piece.

What the photo shows is the joy a man takes in car-driving, his casual turning into a bend. He is not looking at the road, he is not looking at the camera, his sun-glasses point somewhere behind the viewer. He is letting the cool little Speedster carry him past, shoots across the square. Later he will pull up outside some café and there will be plenty of parking spaces and it will not be raining.

A car that is right once is always right.
We have not experienced any single situation in which the TT did not look good. But it does sometimes make its environment look bad.

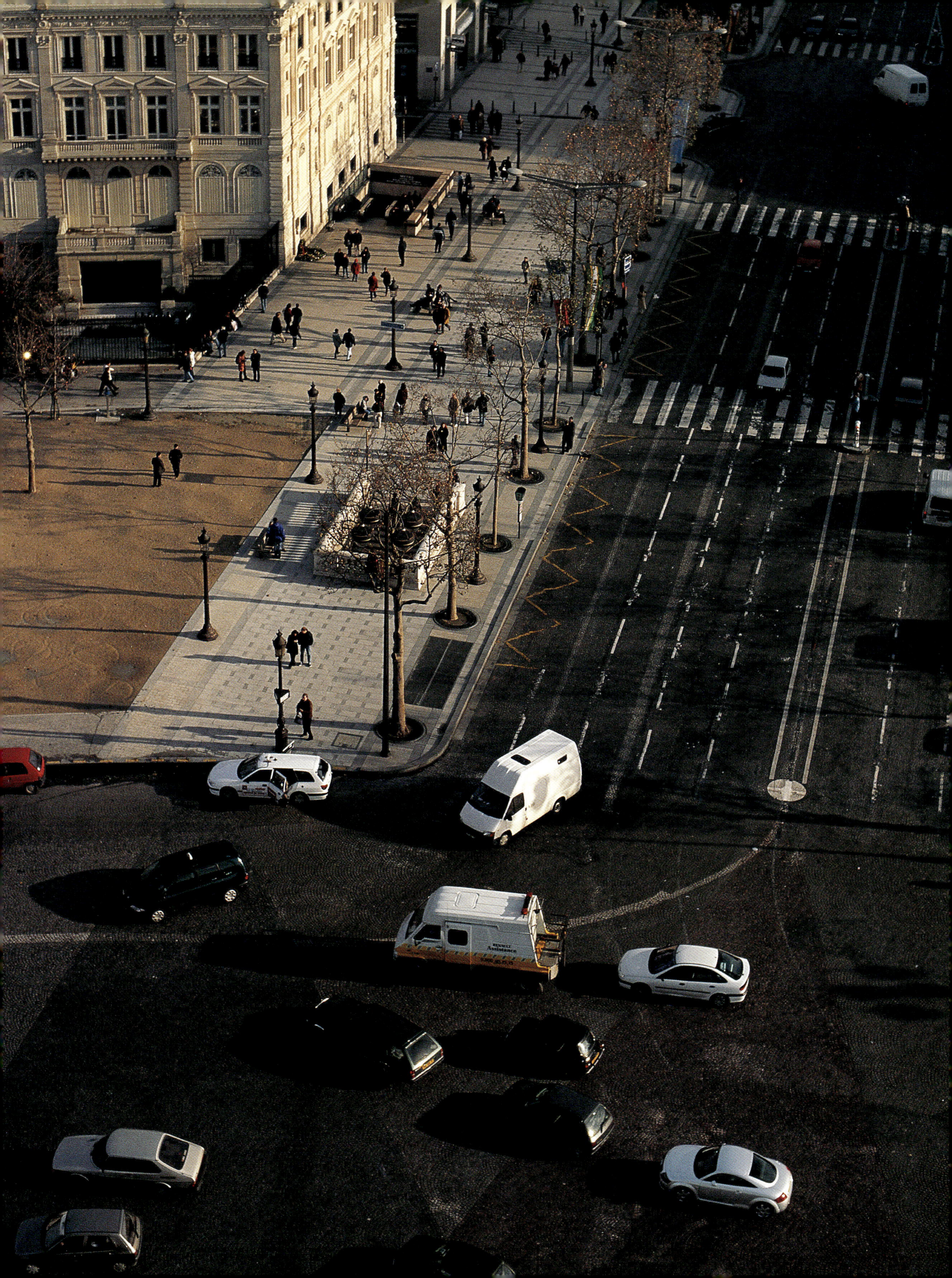

CHERS CLIENTS

POUR UNE BONNE
CIRCULATION

NOUS DEMANDONS
A NOTRE CLIENTELE

**DE NE PAS
STATIONNER**
SUR LE
PONT - BASCULE

MERCI

SORTIE

JOUR
ET NUIT

5935 YR 51

Tête à tête

After a thorough study of the advertised collections, it becomes clear that...

... the TT is now also one of the headwear items which cannot be improved at all in any way.

Paris

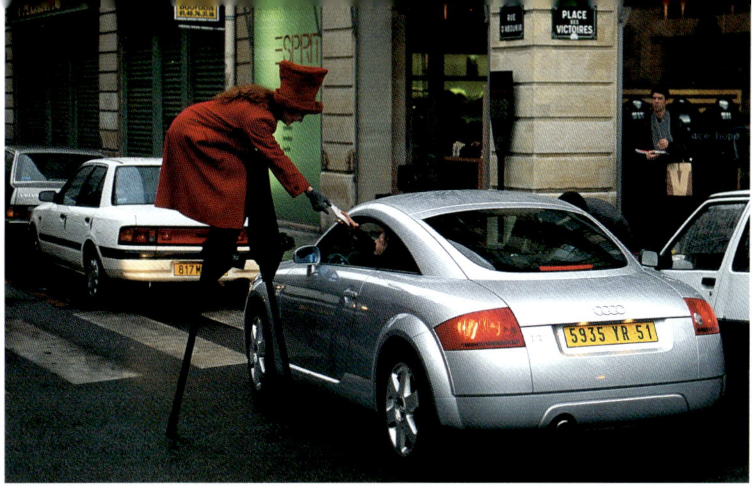
ESPRIT
PLACE
VICTOIRES
5935 YR 51

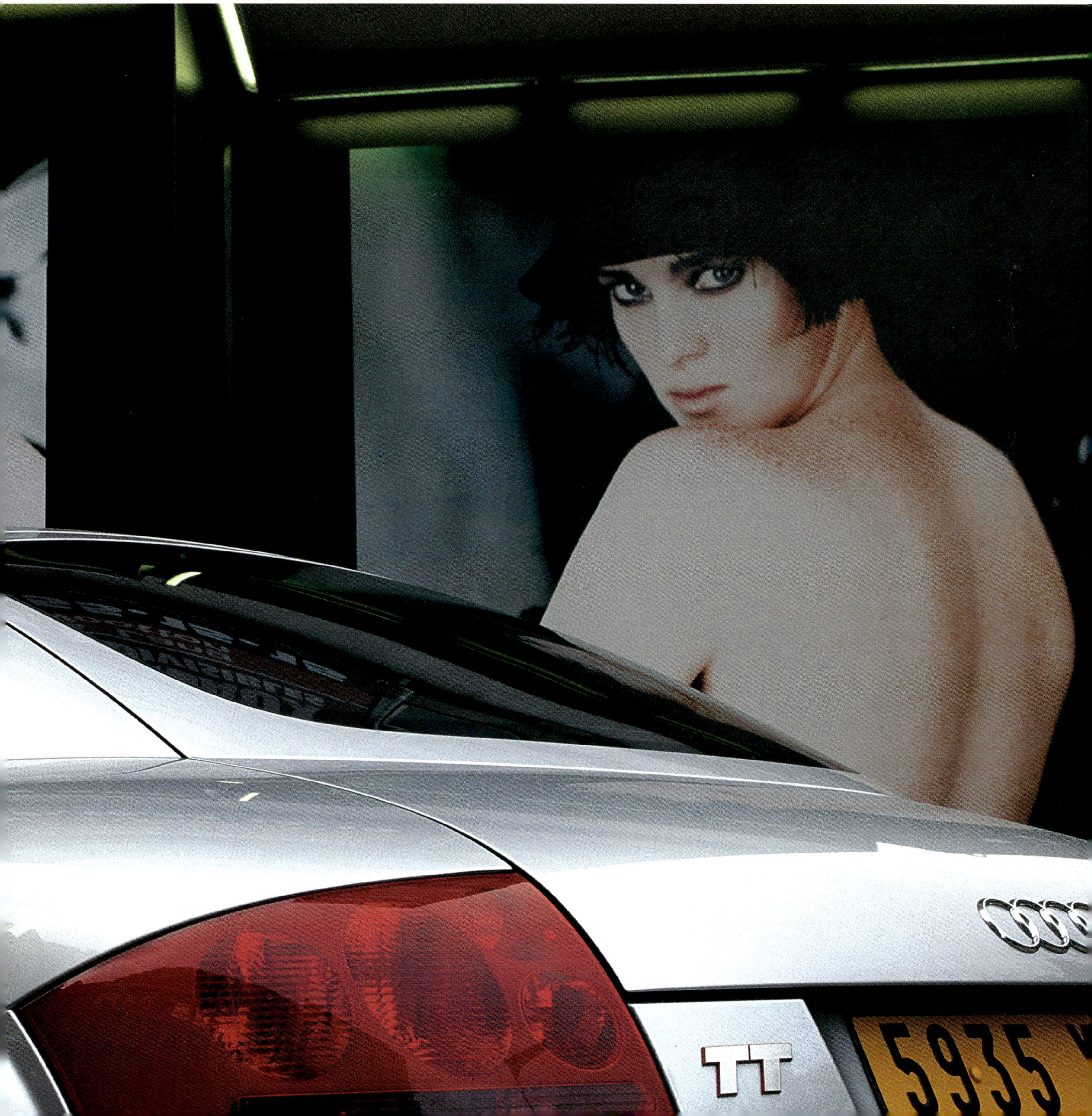
TT
5935

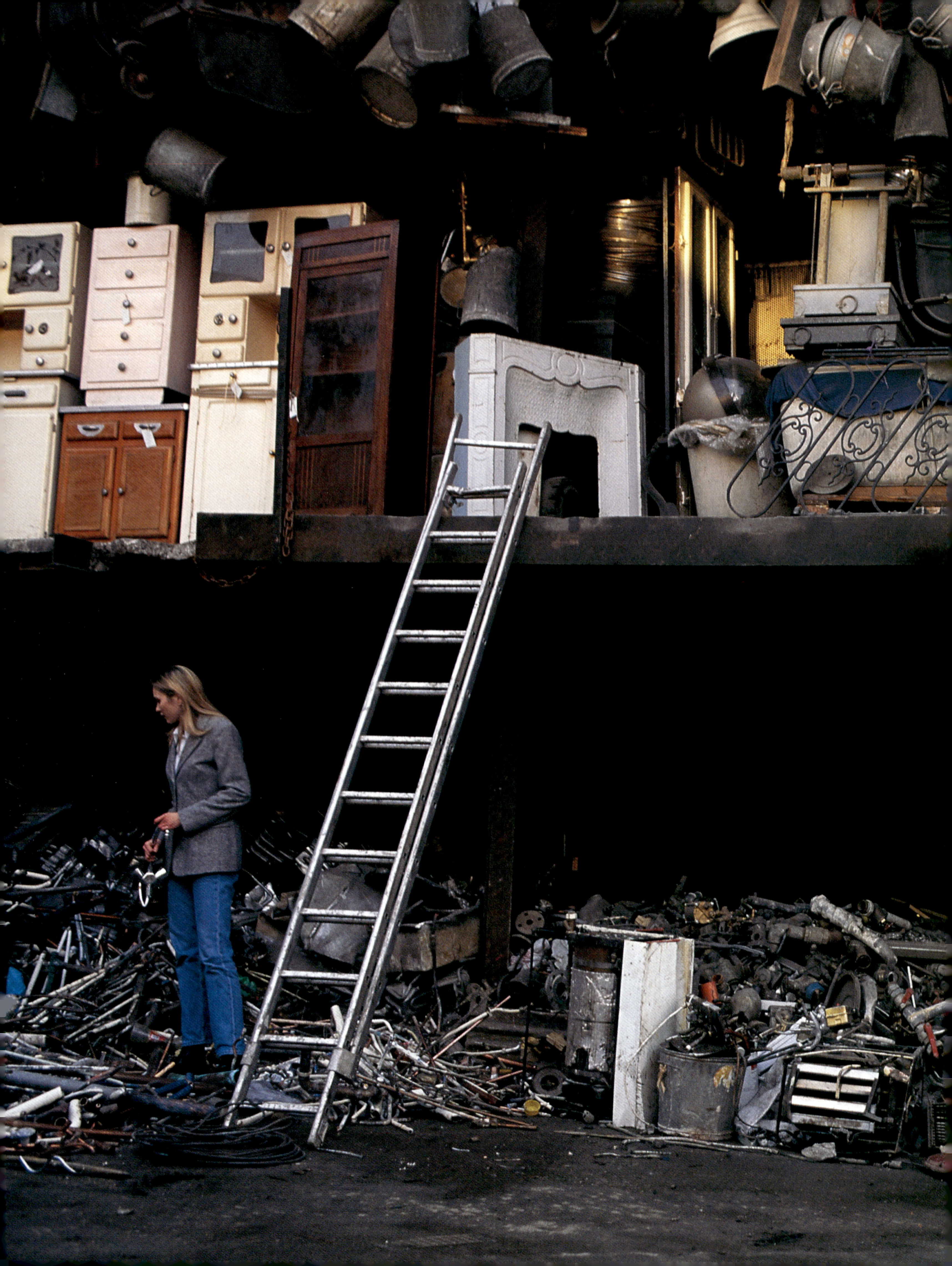

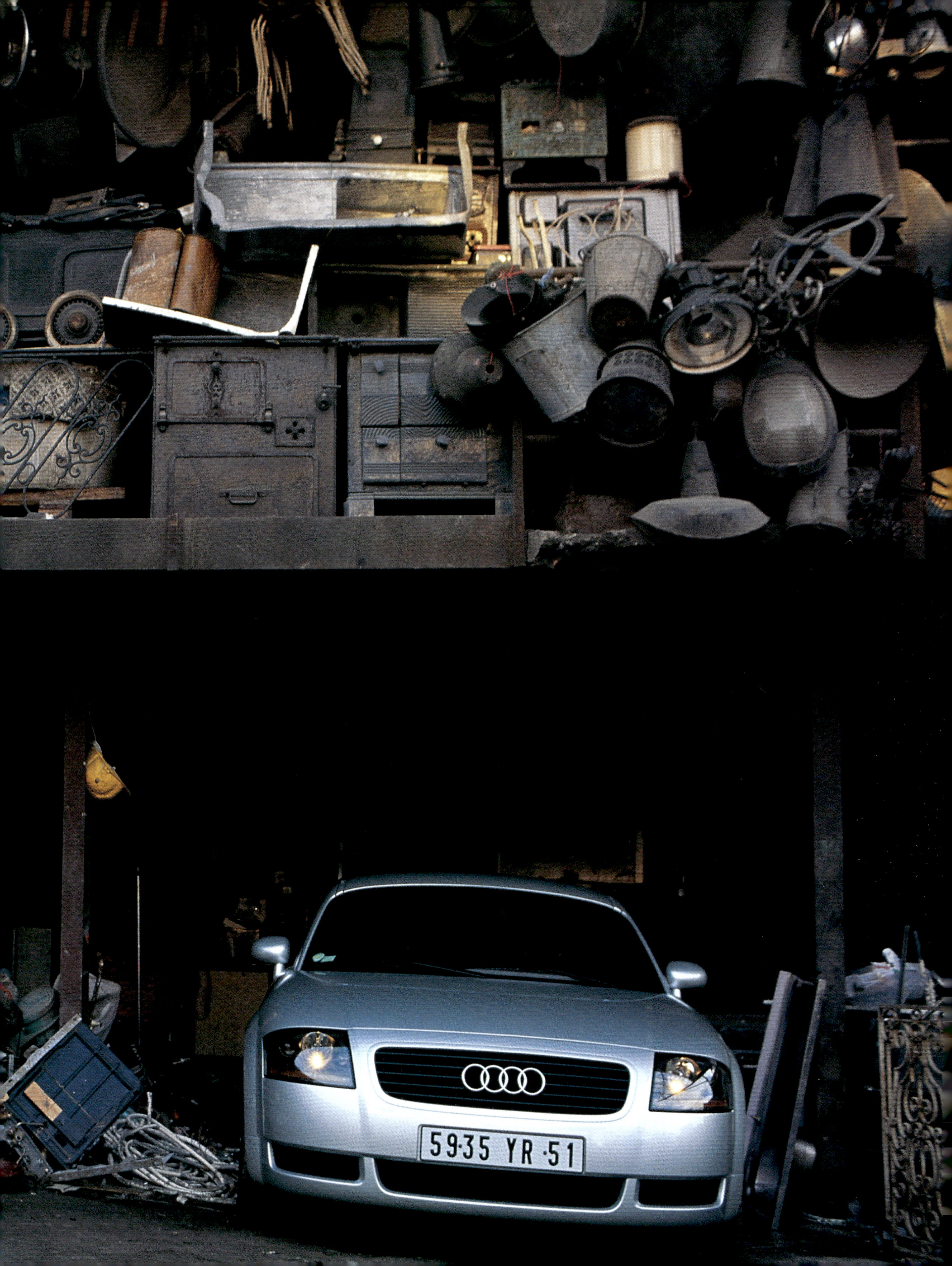
5935 YR 51

Oh, God, here comes
that roundabout nightmare again, which every Paris visitor fears. Good to be sitting in a car which does not anticipate any convex shapes.
ESSENCE?
How did they know that an Audi TT was coming?

Paris

Courtyard window

Bruce will order a strong little coffee and think about a road song leaving room for a girl in the passenger seat. Her dress is like a breath of wind in the hills of Nebraska, but her heart belongs to a whisky smuggler.

The TT is the same sort of nucleus – a compact pressure chamber of opportunities, a concentrated tool of poetry, always cool, unobtrusive – a statement of applied joy in life, not to be confused with fun.

It is inconceivable for this car to let routine take its sluggish path. When a TT is driven, stops, turns off or wheels in, it has the imaginary camera of fate and confidence trained on it, directed by no-one other than us ourselves.

Sounds very flowery, but that is the attraction – that such an unadorned car as the TT is completely romantic, that in all its cool pragmatism, it is also a friend of the heart-carvers, the star-gazers and would-be Byrons. The TT addresses a new generation of romantics, who gain more feeling from the tail of this substantial juice-press than from Chris Isaak's voice.

Where this is a lack of beading, waves and trims, there are provocatively sober radii, delicately undercut proportions, honest materials. And the year-two-thousand trim is a grid of cleanly designed narrow joints, along which doors open, lids lift and lights shine. The wheel rims stand gruffly alone, a little pugnacious, a little dissident. Special laws apply here, the driving function prevails and nothing but. Parisian dogs are crazy about it. Or is it the smell of rubber?

In the protected city environment, the TT has an air of being under-used, like a knight who lays his lance across his saddle or a motor-cyclist absent-mindedly dragging one leg behind him.

The TT is a giant reserve for when-it-really-matters, for sprinting, speed, performance, for braking hard and for pleasure in bends. It seems so talented from afar that it exudes a distracted charm in the city, as if it were a little ashamed of its wide-opening boot, its compact parking size, its smooth stop-and-go gifts, its vibration-free cobble-stone driving. As if all this had only happened because it is such a good fellow who rarely says no.

The little traffic-light racer does have one drawback – because you are always the first at the next red light, you have to twist your neck heaven knows how much until it is green again at last.

Cars are far too seldom seen from above.
Have you ever seen the ground plan of a Beetle? Breath-taking! Admittedly, from the top, the TT looks a bit like a slipper, but a classy slipper!

F A C T S

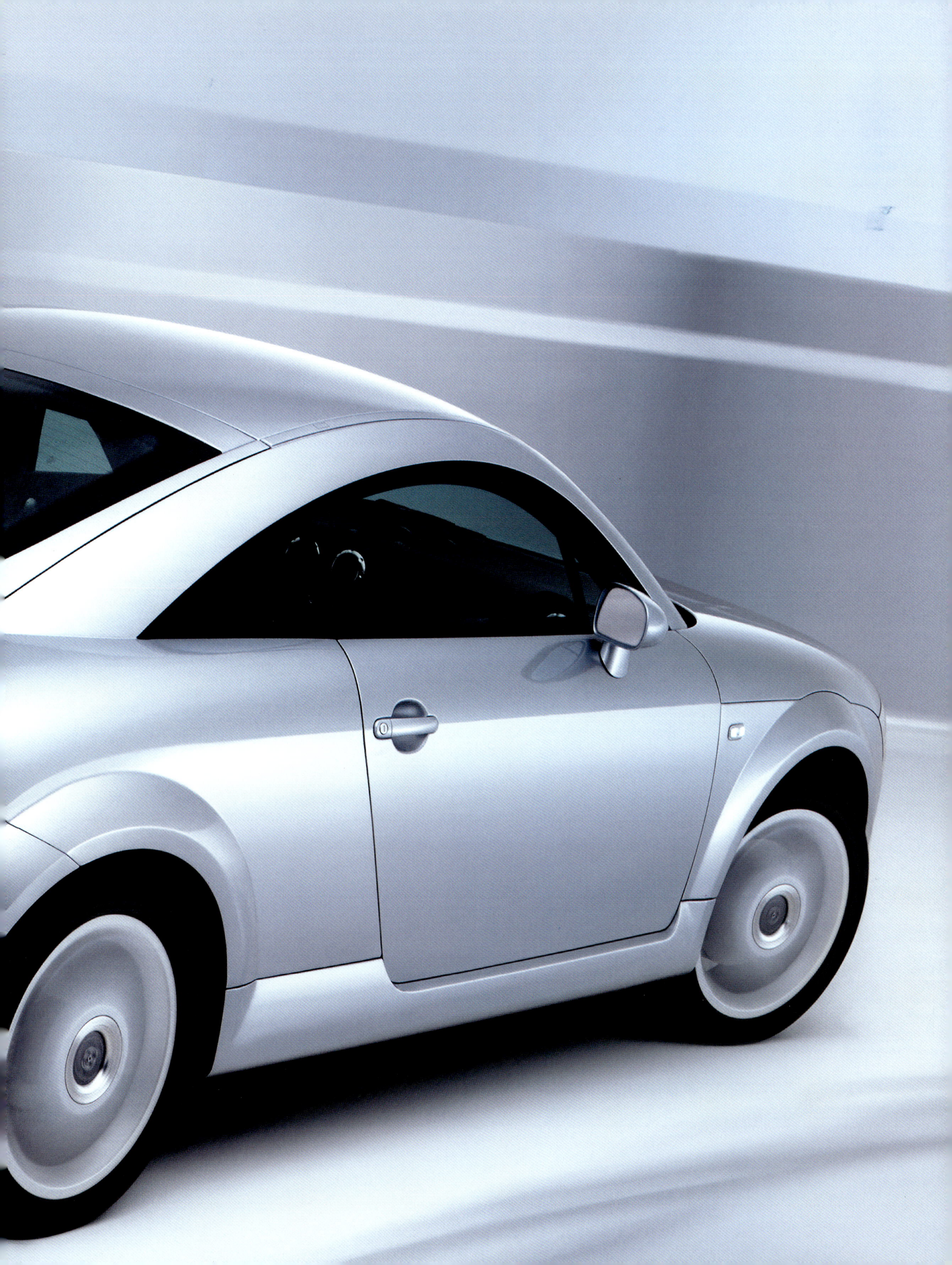

Facts and figures

AUDI TT COUPÉ
(VALUES FOR ROADSTER IN BRACKETS)

Engine/electrics
Four-cylinder spark-ignition with turbocharger and charge-air intercooler, DOHC, hydraulic bucket-type valve tappets, 5 valves per cylinder; displacement 1781 cc, bore 81 mm, stroke 86.4 mm, compression ratio 9.5:1, output 132 kW (180 bhp) at 5500/min, max. torque 235 Nm between 1950 and 5000/min. Motronic MW 7.5 (all-electronic, sequential fuel injection with adaptive idle-speed cylinder filling control, accelerator-pump mixture enrichment, fuel cut-off when coasting, adaptive oxygen sensing). Mapped ignition characteristic with solid-state high-tension ignition distribution, adaptive cylinder-selective knock control, intake-air mass measurement, integrated boost pressure control, coordinated engine-torque control system.

Transmission/driveline
Front-wheel drive with ASR, EDL, hydraulically operated single dry plate clutch with asbestos-free linings, 5-speed manual-shift gearbox.

Chassis/steering/brakes
Front: McPherson struts, triangulated lower wishbones, subframe, anti-roll bar.
Rear: torsion-crank axle, tubular anti-roll bar. Maintenance-free power-assisted rack and pinion steering. Diagonally split dual-circuit brakes with ABS/EBD; brake servo; discs front and rear (ventilated at front). 7J x 16 cast aluminium wheels of 5-arm design, 205/55 R 16 W tyres.

Performance/consumption/acoustics
Top speed 228 km/h (223 km/h)
Acceleration 0-100 km/h in 7.5 s (7.9 s).
Fuel grade: Super Plus unleaded, 98 octane (RON); consumption (urban/extraurban/total) in litres per 100 km 11.0/6.4/8.1 (11.1/6.5/8.2). Exterior noise level at a standstill 90 dB, drive-past value 74 dB.

Weights/capacities
Unladen weight 1240 kg (1310 kg), gross weight limit 1625 kg (1610 kg), front axle load limit 940 kg (960 kg), rear axle load limit 735 kg (705 kg).
Fuel tank capacity 55 litres.

Body/dimensions
Load-bearing fully-galvanized steel body with aluminium engine hood; drag coefficient cD = 0.34 (0.36), frontal area A = 1.99 sq. m. Length 4041 mm, width (excl. mirrors) 1764 mm, height 1349 mm, wheelbase 2422 mm, track (front) 1528 mm, track (rear) 1513 mm. Luggage capacity 220 l/490 l with rear seat back folded (180 l).

1.8-litre five-valve turbocharged engine
with charge-air intercooler and variable camshaft control

1781 cc
134 kW (180 bhp) at 5500/min
235 Nm from 1950 to 5000/min

03/99

The Audi TT is not only convincing for its agile road behaviour and its individualistic lines, but also because of its engine's high, flat torque curve from 1950 to 5000/min, which permits a relaxed style of driving with few gear changes if preferred.

Facts

Audi TT Roadster quattro
Das Fahrwerk
Running gear
03/99

Topless and on all fours – a far from customary combination of virtues for the Audi TT Roadster quattro. The customer's choice is then only between the 180 and 225 bhp engines.

Facts

Technical data

**AUDI TT COUPÉ QUATTRO 180 BHP
(VALUES FOR ROADSTER IN BRACKETS)**

Engine/electrics
Four-cylinder spark-ignition with turbocharger and charge-air intercooler, DOHC, hydraulic bucket-type valve tappets, 5 valves per cylinder; displacement 1781 cc, bore 81 mm, stroke 86.4 mm, compression ratio 9.5:1, output 132 kW (180 bhp) at 5500/min, max. torque 235 Nm between 1950 and 5000/min. Motronic MW 7.5 (all-electronic, sequential fuel injection with adaptive idle-speed cylinder filling control, accelerator-pump mixture enrichment, fuel cut-off when coasting, adaptive oxygen sensing). Mapped ignition characteristic with solid-state high-tension ignition distribution, adaptive cylinder-selective knock control, intake-air mass measurement, integrated boost pressure control, coordinated engine-torque control system.

Transmission/driveline
Permanent four-wheel drive with hydraulic inter-axle clutch, EDS at front, hydraulically operated single dry plate clutch with asbestos-free linings, 5-speed manual-shift gearbox.

Chassis/steering/brakes
Front: McPherson struts, triangulated lower wishbones, subframe, anti-roll bar.
Rear: trailing links and double wishbones, subframe, gas-filled shock absorbers.
Maintenance-free power-assisted rack and pinion steering. Diagonally split dual-circuit brakes with ABS/EBD; brake servo; discs front and rear (ventilated at front). 7J x 16 cast aluminium wheels of 5-arm design, 205/55 R 16 W tyres.

Performance/consumption/acoustics
Top speed 226 km/h (223 km/h)
Acceleration 0-100 km/h in 7.5 s (7.9 s).
Fuel grade: Super Plus unleaded, 98 octane (RON); consumption (urban/extraurban/total) in litres per 100 km 12.8/6.8/9.0 (11.1/6.5/8.2).
Exterior noise level at a standstill 90 dB (86 dB), drive-past value 74 dB.

Weights/capacities
Unladen weight 1340 kg (1310 kg), gross weight limit 1725 kg (1610 kg), front axle load limit 955 kg (960 kg), rear axle load limit 835 kg (705 kg).
Fuel tank capacity 62 litres.

Body/dimensions
Load-bearing fully-galvanized steel body with aluminium engine hood; drag coefficient cD = 0.34 (0.36), frontal area A = 1.99 sq. m. Length 4041 mm, width (excl. mirrors) 1764 mm, height 1348 mm, wheelbase 2429 mm, track (front) 1528 mm, track (rear) 1505 mm. Luggage capacity 220 l/490 l with rear seat back folded (180 l).

Like a sculpture – and maybe soon the Audi TT Coupé could have a place of honour in a design museum (photo at bottom of left page).

Technical data

When power is demanded, the TT can be obtained in either open or closed form with a 225 bhp engine. Here too the absolutely flat torque curve between 2200 and 5500/min is a most welcome surprise. With these data to call upon, the Roadster sprints from 0 to 100 km/h in only 6.7 seconds, and meets its match in terms of aerodynamic and rolling resistance only with 237 km/h on the speedometer.

AUDI TT COUPÉ QUATTRO 225 BHP
(VALUES FOR ROADSTER IN BRACKETS)

Engine/electrics
Four-cylinder spark-ignition with turbo-charger and two charge-air intercoolers, DOHC, hydraulic bucket-type valve tappets, 5 valves per cylinder; displacement 1781 cc, bore 81 mm, stroke 86.4 mm, compression ratio 9.0:1, output 165 kW (225 bhp) at 5900/min, max. torque 280 Nm between 2200 and 5500/min. Motronic ME 7.5 (all-electronic, sequential fuel injection with adaptive idle-speed cylinder filling control, accelerator-pump mixture enrichment, fuel cut-off when coasting, adaptive oxygen sensing). Mapped ignition characteristic with solid-state high-tension ignition distribution, adaptive cylinder-selective knock control, intake-air mass measurement, integrated boost pressure control, coordinated engine-torque control system.

Transmission/driveline
Permanent four-wheel drive with hydraulic inter-axle clutch, EDS at front, hydraulically operated single dry plate clutch with asbestos-free linings, 6-speed manual-shift gearbox.

Chassis/steering/brakes
Front: McPherson struts, triangulated lower wishbones, subframe, anti-roll bar.
Rear: trailing links and double wishbones, subframe, gas-filled shock absorbers.
Maintenance-free power-assisted rack and pinion steering. Diagonally split dual-circuit brakes with ABS/EBD; brake servo; ventilated discs front and rear. 7.5J x 17 cast aluminium wheels of 6-arm design, 225/45 R 17 Y tyres.

Performance/consumption/acoustics
Top speed 243 km/h (237 km/h)
Acceleration 0-100 km/h in 6.4 s (6.7 s).
Fuel grade: Super Plus unleaded, 98 octane (RON); consumption (urban/extraurban/total) in litres per 100 km 12.4/7.4/9.3 (12.6/7.6/9.4).
Exterior noise level at a standstill 87 dB, drive-past value 73 dB.

Weights/capacities
Unladen weight 1395 kg (1460 kg), gross weight limit 1780kg (1760 kg), front axle load limit 1015 kg (1020 kg), rear axle load limit 850 kg (830 kg).
Fuel tank capacity 62 litres.

Body/dimensions
Load-bearing fully-galvanized steel body with aluminium engine hood; drag coefficient cD = 0.34 (0.37), frontal area A = 1 99 sq. m. Length 4041 mm, width (excl. mirrors) 1764 mm, height 1348 mm, wheelbase 2429 mm, track (front) 1528 mm, track (rear) 1505 mm. Luggage capacity 220 l/490 l with rear seat back folded (180 l).

1.8-litre five-valve turbocharged engine
with two charge-air intercoolers and variable camshaft control
1781 cc
165 kW (225 bhp) at 5900/min
280 Nm from 2200 to 5500/min
03/99

Facts

Lifestyle

By Monika Lewandowski

What takes your fancy?

FOR THE BROCKHAUS ENCYCLOPAEDIA – that fountain of all knowledge so widely read in all German-speaking countries – the concept of the "lifestyle product" is obviously too new. Even "Accessories" only rates two lines: "Fashionable accompanying items such as belts, jewellery and gloves." Is that all? A modern definition ought to go a long way farther than that.

Lifestyle products now encompass a whole catalogue of articles produced all over the world by highly specialised suppliers. The quality standard can clearly differ quite considerably: it's surely unfair to put a mass-produced plastic ball pen into the same category as a skilfully crafted wristwatch, and the same criteria apply to the anoraks, scarves and leather caps offered to the enthusiastic roadster driver or passenger. Nor can the automobile manufacturer risk omitting a good range of scale models from its lifestyle products list, since these are very popular items – though here again surprises can't be ruled out, as we shall see shortly.

A big range of products, in other words, which are clearly of interest to equally large numbers of customers of both sexes who either identify closely with the Audi marque or are quite simply impressed by the quality and style of these products. Ideally, of course, both these customer attributes come together and culminate in a powerful desire to purchase and own them.

A car such as the TT, with its own very marked character, naturally needs a range of lifestyle products that bears the same individual stamp. For Peter Schreyer there is no doubt that "our designers must have a word or two to say about the appearance of the lifestyle products, and to ensure that the TT Coupé's or TT Roadster's styling philosophy is reflected in every design area."

This starts with form and design, but the designers also take a look at the materials before they commit themselves to a favourable verdict. For Romulus Rost, therefore, it was clear from the outset that watches bearing the TT

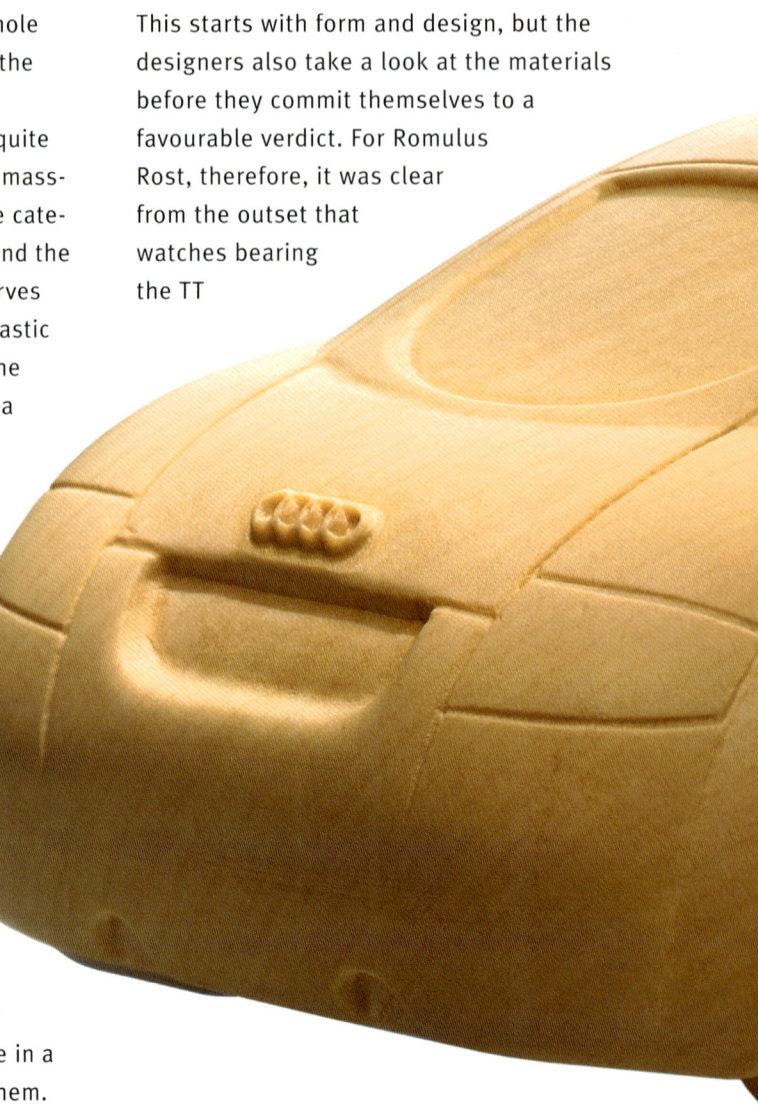

A pleasure to handle:
a wooden TT model entirely made from solid oiled maple

label would have to possess that certain "feeling" that his "aluminium interior" communicates so effectively: "A neatly laid out dial and correctly located control buttons that are pleasant to operate – all packed in a stylish, rounded form. How else could a watch closely related to the TT possibly look?"

Lifestyle product design, therefore, clearly has to be based closely on the main product. In the case of the watch, the matt-finished stainless steel case is intended to recall the aluminium ring used at various points on the dash panel. It fascinates the senses of sight and touch just like, for example, the car's ventilation outlets, and creates a strong urge to feel and to hold it as often as possible.

The watches naturally have to comply with all the other strict criteria that an Audi product is expected to fulfil – and therefore they are made in the home-country of the world's finest watches, in other words they are "Swiss made".

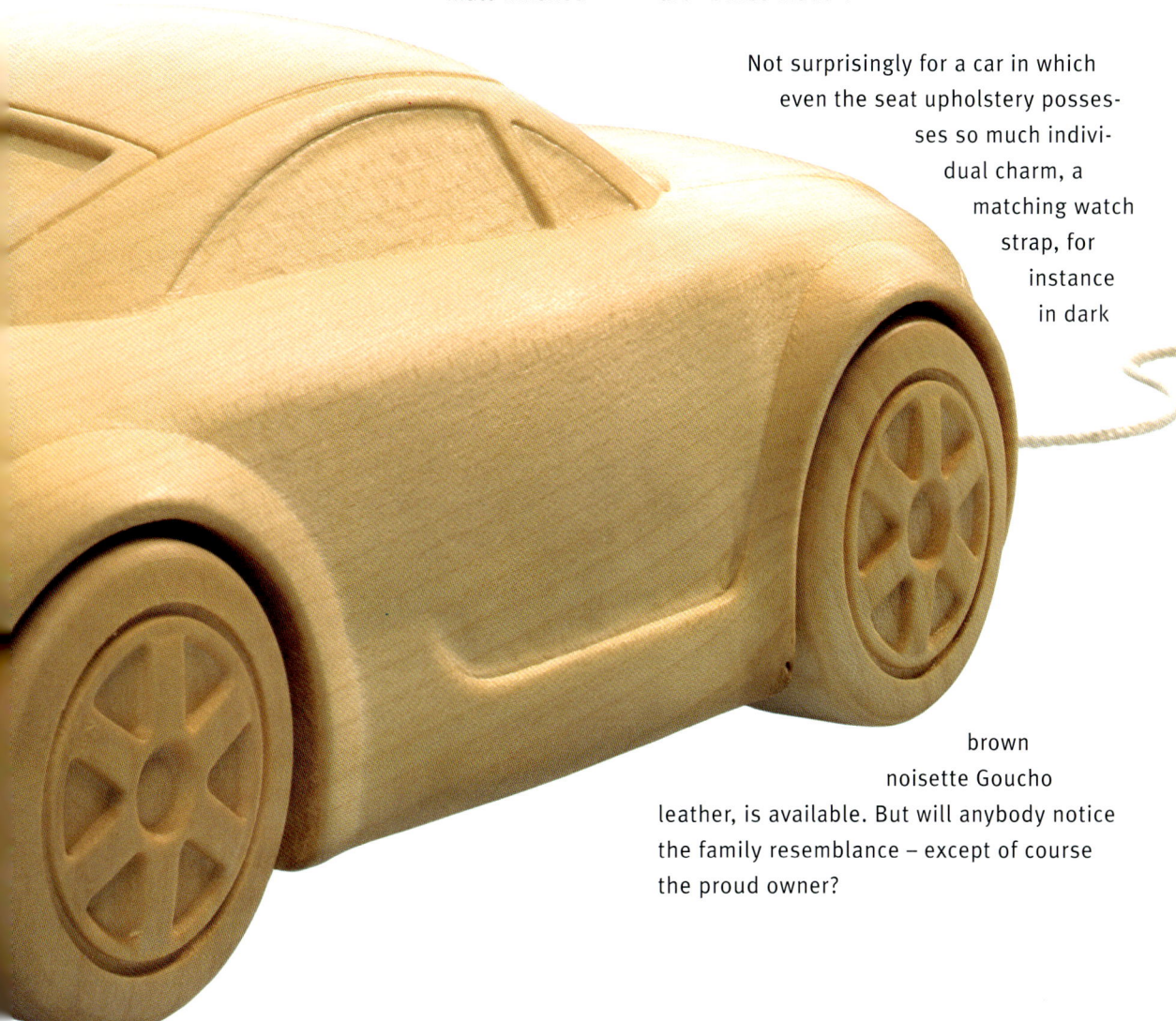

Not surprisingly for a car in which even the seat upholstery possesses so much individual charm, a matching watch strap, for instance in dark brown noisette Goucho leather, is available. But will anybody notice the family resemblance – except of course the proud owner?

Lifestyle

Swiss made, of course: the watches with the TT look communicate a very strong "TT feeling".

But didn't we make a passing reference to scale-model cars earlier? This is precisely the area in which Audi's designers and the company's lifestyle products team have created the gem of the collection: a pull-along toy car made from solid maple wood, with an oiled surface. Almost twenty-five centimetres long, it's ideal for pulling along behind you on a string – an amusement that either children or grown-ups with a residually juvenile attitude to life should not allow themselves to miss.

Here too, the technical aspects of the design are flawless. What would be the value of Audi's celebrated 'Vorsprung durch Technik' slogan if this were not so? The wheels revolve smoothly, particularly on parquet floors. This is not the surface that shows off the car's noise insulation at its best, but it certainly attracts attention. The real pleasure, however, is to feel the superb surface of this solid-wood model.

As distinguished as the TT itself: luggage made specially for the TT.

(Incidentally, did you know that the maple is a member of the *acer* genus of trees that are to be found in Europe, temperate areas of Asia and North America?)

To hold the wooden TT in one's hands is to feel an irresistible urge to stroke it, but one should also take time out to admire the sheer skill of the "Herrgottschnitzer", the local craftsmen who carve religious figures in Italy's Grödner Valley or Val Gardena.

With this provenance it is only correct for each car to have the craftsman's name carved on the underside, together with the place where it was made.

Each of these "toy" cars – may we be excused the term – is therefore a unique masterpiece. As an adult member of society, admittedly, it is probably too unusual to be seen carrying – or towing – such an article around. An Audi men's watch is surely a more appropriate choice. So don't forget: the watch for when you're on the move, the wooden car to amuse and delight you at home. Unless your kids insist on taking the "maple wood TT" with them on your next journey in a "real" Audi.

TT enthusiasts will soon discover that telling the time TT-style is not the whole of life. Tours, visits and outings large and small are an even greater pleasure with suitable clothing and luggage in one's possession. The highly reputable House of Bogner, for example, supplies jackets, gloves and luggage for inclusion in the TT's lifestyle product catalogue. The choice of this supplier, renowned for many years for the clearly defined, fashionable cut of its garments, emphasises the exclusive character that Audi has sought even for products that could be dismissed prematurely as high-class trivia.

Audi also offers women's Paisley scarves made from a silk and linen blend; their fashionable elegance is highly convincing. For the allegedly stronger sex, there are scarves in the TT lifestyle product programme woven from a wool and alpaca blend, with a slightly more formal chessboard pattern.

Lifestyle

The authors and the publishers thank Audi AG for its invaluable help and support, without which a book such as this could never have been produced.

Their special thanks are due to the Chairman of the Board of Management, Dr. Franz-Josef Paefgen, to Dr. Werner Mischke, the Board member responsible for Technical Affairs and Development, to Project Leaders Dr. Ulrich Hackenberg and Stefan Härdl and to the Head of Audi Design, Peter Schreyer, all of whom answered even the most unusual questions with immense patience.

The authors also express their thanks to Rudolf Schiller (Communication/Technical Affairs), Jörg Ellhof (Advertising/Classic Media), Thomas Frank (Public Relations/Communication), Rainer Nistl (Manager, Public Affairs), Romulus Rost and Freeman Thomas (Design), Ralf-Gerhard Willner (Technical Development) and Ralph Schollähn (Design Communication).

Trade marks reproduced by kind permission of AUDI AG, Ingolstadt Editor: AUDI AG, Public Affairs, Ingolstadt

1st Edition © 1999 Delius, Klasing & Co., Bielefeld

Supervision: Audi Design Design: Uli Praetor Layout: Andreas Hemm, Kerstin Kerle Fotos: Peter Vann and AUDI AG archives English translations: Colin Brazier and AUDI Akademie (chapters "Iceland" and "Paris") Editorial assistance: Monika Lewandowski

*Contributions by:
Jürgen Lewandowski:
Signs/A Discussion with Dr. Franz-Josef Paefgen
Design/In the Beginning was the Idea
The TT: Classical, Visionary/Breathing Life into a New Car
The Commuter/A TT is Always on the Move
Those Days in Paris/A TT is a TT, an Apple is a Pomme
Shown in the USA/TheTT or 100 Percent Audi
Herbert Völker:
Iceland/The Story of the Launch Photos
David Staretz:
The Sparrow of Paris/A Car that the City Loves
Monika Lewandowski:
Lifestyle Products/What Takes your Fancy?*

Blockmaking: Service vor dem Druck, Bielefeld Printing: Kunst- und Werbedruck, Bad Oeynhausen Printed in Germany 1999

All rights reserved. Rights for the use of the illustrations lie with AUDI AG, for the text contributions with the publishing house. This publication is not to be reproduced, transmitted or otherwise copied either wholly or in part, whether manually or by electronic or manual means, including photocopying, recording on tape or storage of data, unless express permission has first been obtained.

Delius Klasing Verlag, Siekerwall 21, D-33602 Bielefeld Tel.: 0521/559-0, Fax: 0521/559-113 e-mail: info@delius-klasing.de http://www.delius-klasing.de